The Official Rules of Chess

Professional, Scholastic, Amateur & Internet Chess Rules

ABOUT THE AUTHORS

Eric Schiller, widely considered one of the world's foremost chess writers and teachers, is internationally recognized for his definitive works on chess. He is the author of 100 chess books including *World Champion Openings*, *Standard Chess Openings*, and *Unorthodox Chess Openings*—an exhaustive opening library of more than 1700 pages – as well as *Encyclopedia of Chess Wisdom,* and *639 Essential Endgame Positions.* Schiller is a National and Life Master, an International Arbiter of F.I.D.E., and the official trainer for many of America's top young players. Schiller was the arbiter of the 2000 Braingames World Championship match between Kasparov and Kramnik and has been involved with organizing World Championship and other major chess events for over 20 years.

Richard Peterson is the Executive Director of the Chess Education Association and is generally regarded as the nation's leading scholastic chess organizer. Peterson has coached individuals and teams to 30 national scholastic chess championships including 11 consecutive years with at least one national champion. His students have made a dozen All America teams and have represented the United States seven times at the world youth championships. His daughter Andrea was the first girl national scholastic chess champion and his son David won a record nine national championships. Richard and his children were featured in the movie *Chess Kids*.

Arbiters Schiller and Reuben at the 2000 Braingames World Championship

The Official Rules of Chess

Professional, Scholastic, Amateur & Internet Chess Rules

ERIC SCHILLER
and
RICHARD PETERSON

CARDOZA PUBLISHING

FIRST EDITION

Library of Congress: 00-131806 • ISBN 1-58042-025-7

Write for your free catalogue of gaming and chess books,
equipment, software and computer games.

CARDOZA PUBLISHING
PO Box 1500, Cooper Station, New York NY 10276
Phone (718)743-5229 • Fax (718)743-8284
Email: Cardozapub@aol.com
Web Site: www.cardozapub.com

PREFACE

This new rulebook updates the standard rules of chess for the new millennium, providing the official rules used in World Championship, scholastic, amateur and online competitions. The rules presented here were used in the 2000 Braingames.net World Chess Championship (main rules), Chess Education Association 2000 Championships (main rules and scholastic rules) and in competitions at the Internet Chess Club. They are the standard rules of chess, substantially the same as the rules used by the World Chess Federation (FIDE) with a few technological updates.

In addition to the actual rules, we present important advice on chess equipment, etiquette, the duties and responsibilities of the arbiters, codes of conduct for parents and coaches, and information on chess tournaments.

All in all, we hope you will find all the information needed to play chess at the school, amateur, professional and even World Championship level. Some of this information will change over time, so we recommend that you visit our website www.chesscity.com to keep abreast of new developments.

The rules presented in this book were worked out by many top players and arbiters. The authors wish to acknowledge the valuable contributions of the following individuals:

14th World Champion Vladimir Kramnik (Russia)
13th World Champion Garry Kasparov (Russia)
Grandmaster and International Arbiter Yuri Averbakh (Russia)
Grandmaster and International Arbiter Raymond Keene (England)
Grandmaster and International Arbiter Lothar Schmid (Germany)
Grandmaster Miguel Illescas Cordoba (Spain)
International Master and Arbiter Andrzej Filipowicz (Poland)
International Arbiter Vladimir Dvorkovich (Russia)
International Arbiter Stewart Reuben (England)

TABLE OF CONTENTS

VIII. Time Controls 50

IX. Chess Rating Systems 54

X. Chess Teachers, Coaches and Trainers 58

XI. The Tournament Director 65

XII. Responsibilities of the Players 68

XIII. The Chess Education Association 69

IV. Selected Resources   79

Appendix A: Pairing Systems   82

Appendix B: Braingames.net World Chess Championship Regulations   86

Appendix C: A Few Words on USCF Rules   93

Last Words   95

I. INTRODUCTION

The standard rules of chess have been around for well over a century, undergoing minor modifications from time to time. The vast majority of chess tournaments are played under these rules, as are most casual and online games. At the dawn of the new millennium, it is appropriate that the various rules for serious, casual, scholastic and online chess be collected into one reference book so that all chess players can have a clear understanding of the rules.

We concentrate on the basics: rules, etiquette and standards which can be used in any chess competition. Our goal is to present the official and best rules actually used in competitions.

The first section of the book is devoted to the rules of play and basic tournament rules, including the correct method of recording moves. While there are still a few organizations that adopt their own set of rules, following the rules as presented here will almost always keep a player out of trouble. A few exceptions involving the unorthodox rules of the United States Chess Federation are discussed at the end of the book.

With the general rules out of the way, we will turn to specific exceptions for scholastic chess, taking into account the capabilities of young players. Some kids learn chess before they can read and write, so chess notation and complex rules need to be eliminated. The basic rules of the game are unchanged, however. These rules can also be applied to amateur chess, but there are a few additional considerations for competitions among amateurs, both adults and children. The development of online chess has simplified some matters (it is not necessary to write down the moves when playing online, as the software records the game) but additional ethical questions arise. We'll provide interpretations based on years of experience at the Internet Chess Club.

We will also discuss appropriate etiquette for players, teachers, coaches, trainers, and even parents. While this advice is not part of the technical rules, the reader is advised to treat the standards of etiquette just as seriously in order to be a good standing member of the chess community.

There are many different types of chess competitions, from informal games in the park to online games, right on up to the World

Championship itself. While the technical details of the tournaments and rating systems lie outside the scope of this book, we'll present the basics without complex mathematical formulae and algorithms. It is important to understand the principles of the pairing systems used in most tournaments, as this is where the majority of disputes arise. Unfortunately, there are no standard rules, and even when a local organization or national federation has strict guidelines, tournament directors often stray from the designated path. We'll provide the understanding necessary to evaluate the pairing systems during tournament play.

An entire section is devoted to the Chess Education Association, a governing body for chess played in the schools. This information will be particularly valuable to parents, coaches and school officials.

Finally, just to give a picture of the complexity of running a chess event with professional players, we add the technical regulations of the 2000 Braingames.net World Championship. You might find some of these rules picky to the point of being amusing, but with millions of dollars on the line, the players insist on clear interpretations of even minor details.

We have avoided indulging in personal interpretations of the rules in order not to blur the line between the rules themselves and our particular interpretations when working as arbiter or tournament director of a chess tournament. As with baseball umpires, the "strike zone" may vary. Serious tournaments have procedures in place to appeal rulings by arbiters and directors, and in many circumstances the officials have a wide degree of latitude. There are some who prefer a system based on precedent, as in law, but in our experience precedent is only a guideline. Any good sport official can tell you that sometimes you have to act based on your knowledge of an individual player and the precise circumstances of a rule infraction.

Just as the various types of chess competitions vary in formality, so does our presentation. The official rules are, like any set of regulations, a bit dry. That is necessary, since they form the basis of rulings which can affect players deeply. As we move to the less formal topics of scholastic and amateur chess, and matters of etiquette, you'll find the reading more pleasurable, we hope.

II. THE OFFICIAL RULES OF CHESS

The following are the standard rules of chess as applied in World Championship competition. In a later chapter we present some of the variations of the rules used in amateur, scholastic, and online competitions. These rules conform in most part to those of the world chess federation (FIDE), but differ significantly from those found in American tournaments conducted under the auspices of the United States Chess Federation. Since most American tournaments are amateur events, those rules are discussed in the section on amateur rules.

This set of rules was composed by International Arbiter Eric Schiller, with the cooperation and valuable assistance of International Arbiters Andrzej Filipowicz (Poland) and Yuri Averbakh (Russia). They were used verbatim in the 2000 Braingames.net World Chess Championship and were personally approved by World Champion Garry Kasparov and his challenger Vladimir Kramnik. Additional advice was provided by Lothar Schmid of Germany, the International Arbiter who oversaw the Fischer vs. Spassky matches in 1972 and 1992.

SCOPE

The Rules of Chess cannot cover all possible situations that may arise during a game. The Arbiter's judgment will apply when there is no specific rule available.

RULES OF PLAY

Article 1: The Nature & Objectives of the Game of Chess

1.1. The game of chess is played between two opponents who move pieces alternately on a square board called a *chessboard*. The player who has control of the white pieces (White) starts the game. A player is said to 'have the move', when the opponent's move has been completed.

1.2. The objective of each player is to arrive at a position such that the opponent's king has no legal move which would avoid the capture of the king on the following move. This situation is called *checkmate* and the player who checkmates his opponent wins the game. The player who has been checkmated loses the game.

Article 2: The Initial Position of the Pieces on the Chessboard

2.1. The chessboard is composed of an 8 x 8 grid of 64 equal alternating light and dark squares. The chessboard is placed between the players in such a way that the near corner square to the right of the player is a light square.

2.2. At the beginning of the game one player has 16 light-colored pieces (the *white* pieces); the other has 16 dark-colored pieces (the *black* pieces). Each side has one king, one queen, two rooks, two bishops, two knights and eight pawns.

2.3. The initial position of the pieces on the chessboard is as follows where the following symbols represent the pieces: ♟= pawn, ♞ = knight, ♝= bishop, ♜ = rook, ♛= queen, ♚= king:

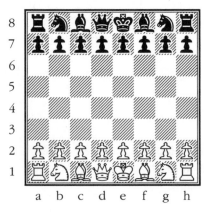

2.4. The eight vertical columns of squares are referred to as *files*. The eight horizontal rows of squares are referred to as *ranks*. A straight line of squares of the same color, touching corner to corner, is referred to as a *diagonal*.

Article 3: The Moves of the Pieces

3.1. No piece can be moved to a square occupied by a piece of the same color (white or black). If a piece moves to a square occupied by an opponent's piece the latter is captured and removed from the chessboard as part of the same move. A piece is said to *attack* a square if the piece could move to that square on the next turn and capture an opponent's piece if one occupies the square.

3.2. (a) The queen moves to any square along the file, the rank or a diagonal on which it stands.

(b) The rook moves to any square along the file or the rank on which it stands.

(c) The bishop moves to any square along a diagonal on which it stands.

When making these moves the queen, rook or bishop cannot move over any intervening pieces.

3.3. The knight moves to one of the squares nearest to that on which it stands but not on the same rank, file or diagonal.

3.4. The pawn has five legal moves:

(a) The pawn moves forward to the unoccupied square immediately in front of it on the same file

(b) On its first move each pawn may advance two squares along the same file provided both squares are unoccupied

(c) The pawn moves to a square occupied by an opponent's piece which is diagonally in front of it on an adjacent file, capturing that piece.

(d) A pawn attacking a square crossed by an opponent's pawn which has advanced two squares in one move from its original square may capture this opponent's pawn as though the latter had been moved only one square. This capture can be made only on the move following this advance and is called an 'en passant' capture.

(e) When a pawn reaches the rank furthest from its starting position it must be exchanged as part of the same move for a queen, rook, bishop or knight of the same color. The player's choice is not restricted to pieces that have been captured previously. This exchange of a pawn for another piece is called 'promotion' and the effect of the new piece is immediate. If the desired piece is not physically available, the player should summon the arbiter, who will provide the piece. Alternatively, the player may use an inverted rook to represent a queen, or may lay the pawn on its side and verbally indicate which piece it represents. If an arbiter is present, the arbiter should replace the inverted rook or pawn with a queen.

3.5. The king can move in two different ways, by:

(a) moving to any adjoining square that is not attacked by one or more of the opponent's pieces, provided that the king is not in check at the conclusion of the move. The king is said to be in *check*, if it is under attack by one or more of the opponent's pieces, even if those opposing pieces cannot themselves move.

(b) *Castling* This is a move of the king and either rook of the same color on the same rank, counting as a single move of the king and executed as follows: the king is transferred from its original square two squares towards the rook, then that rook is transferred over the king to the square the king has just crossed.

Castling is illegal in the following situations:

[i] if the king has already been moved.

[ii] with a rook that has already been moved.

[iii] while the square on which the king stands, or the square which it must cross, or the square which it is to occupy, is attacked by one or more of the opponent's pieces.

[iv] while there is any piece between the king and the rook with which castling is to be effected.

Article 4: The Act of Moving the Pieces

4.1. Each move must be made with one hand only.

4.2. Provided that he first expresses the intention (e.g. by saying *adjust*), the player having the move may adjust one or more pieces on their squares.

4.3. Except as provided in Article 4.2, if the player having the move deliberately touches one or more of either player's pieces on the chessboard, the first piece touched must be moved or captured, if the resulting move is legal. If a player touches one piece belonging to each side, the opponent's piece must be captured using the player's own touched piece, or, if this is illegal, move or capture the first piece touched which can be moved or captured. If it is unclear, the player's own piece shall be considered to have been touched before the opponent's.

4.4. (a) If a player deliberately touches the king and a rook he must castle on that side if it is legal.

(b) If a player deliberately touches a rook and then the king he is not allowed to castle on that side on that move and the situation shall be governed by Article 4.3.

(c) If a player intending to castle, touches the king or king and a rook at the same time, but castling on that side is illegal, the player must choose either to castle on the other side, provided that castling on that side is legal, or to move the king. If the king has no legal move, the player is free to make any legal move.

4.5. If none of the pieces touched can be moved or captured, the player may make any legal move.

4.6. If the opponent violates Article 4.3 or 4.4, the player cannot claim this after he himself deliberately touches a piece.

4.7. When a piece has been released on a square, it cannot then be moved to another square, and the turn is completed. The move is considered to be made when all the relevant requirements of Article 3 have been fulfilled.

Article 5: The Completed Game

5.1. (a) The game is won by the player who has checkmated the opponent's king with a legal move. This immediately ends the game.

(b) The game is won by the player whose opponent *resigns*. Resignation takes place when the opponent either verbally informs the player by saying "I resign" or who indicates resignation on the scoresheet by...

[I] Writing the word "resigns" in the space which would normally hold the move to be played.

[ii] Circling the appropriate result.

[iii] Writing "0-1" (in the case that White is resigning) or "1-0" (in the case the Black is resigning) and signs the scoresheet. This immediately ends the game.

5.2. The game is drawn when the player to move has no legal move and the king is not in check. The game is said to end in *stalemate.* This immediately ends the game.

5.3. The game is drawn upon agreement between the two players during the game. This immediately ends the game. (See Article 9.1)

5.4. The game may be drawn if the identical position is about to appear or has appeared on the chessboard three times. (See Article 9.2)

5.5. The game may be drawn if the last 50 consecutive moves have been made by each player without the movement of any pawn and without the capture of any piece. (See Article 9.3)

TOURNAMENT RULES
Article 6: The Chess Clock

6.1. A chess *clock* is a device with two time displays, connected to each other in such a way that only one of them can run at one time. *Clock* in the Rules of Chess means one of the two time displays. *Expiration* means the expiry of the allotted time for a player.

6.2. When using a chess clock, each player must make a certain number or all moves in an allotted period of time; or may be allocated an additional amount of time after each move. The time saved by a player during one period is added to the time available for the next period, except in the *incremental* mode. In the *incremental* mode both players receive an allotted *primary thinking time.* They also receive a *fixed extra time* for every move. The count down of the main time only commences after the fixed time has expired. Provided the player stops the clock before the expiry of the fixed time, the main thinking time does not change, irrespective of the proportion of the fixed time used.

6.3. Each chess clock has a device which indicates when time has expired.

6.4. The arbiter or tournament director determines where the chess clock is placed. In the absence of relevant authority, the clock is placed on the right side of the board, from the perspective of the player of the Black pieces.

6.5. At the time determined for the start of the game the clock of the player who has the white pieces is started by the black player.

6.6. The player shall lose the game if he arrives at the chessboard more than one hour after the scheduled start of the session.

6.7. (a) During the game each player, having made the move on the chessboard, shall stop the clock controlling the player's time and start the opponent's clock. A player must always be allowed to stop the clock. The move is not considered to have been completed until he has done so, unless the made move ends the game. (See Articles 5.1, 5.2 and 5.3)

The time between making the move on the chessboard and stopping the clock and starting the opponent's clock is regarded as part of the time allotted to the player.

(b) A player must stop the clock with the same hand as that with which he made the move. It is forbidden for either player to obstruct the access of the opponent to the clock.

(c) The players must handle the chess clock gently. It is forbidden to punch it forcibly, to pick it up or to knock it over. Improper clock handling shall be penalized in accordance with Article 13.4.

6.8. Expiration of the time control occurs when the arbiter observes the fact or when a valid claim to that effect has been made by either player.

6.9. Except where Articles 5.1, 5.2 and 5.3 apply, if a player does not complete the prescribed number of moves in the allotted time, the game is lost by the player. However, the game is drawn, if the position is such that the opponent cannot checkmate the player by any possible series of legal moves.

6.10. Every indication given by the clocks is considered to be conclusive in the absence of any evident defect. A chess clock with an evident defect shall be replaced. The arbiter shall use best judgment when determining the times to be shown on the replacement chess clock.

6.11. If the clock in use allows both expiration of time on both sides, and it is impossible to establish which player's time expired first, the game shall continue.

6.12. (a) If the game needs to be interrupted, the arbiter shall stop the clocks.

(b) A player may stop the clocks in order to seek the arbiter's assistance.

(c) The arbiter shall decide when the game is to be restarted.

6.13. If an irregularity occurs and/or the pieces have to be restored to a previous position, the arbiter shall determine the times to be shown on the clocks, using the best evidence at available.

6.14. Devices and displays showing the current position on the chessboard, the moves and the number of moves made, and clocks which also show the number of moves, are allowed in the playing hall. However, these devices are not to be considered conclusive evidence in support of any claim, and remain at all times unofficial.

Article 7: Illegal Positions

7.1. (a) If during a game it is found that the initial position of the pieces was incorrect, the game shall be canceled and a new game played.

(b) If during a game it is found that the only error is that the chessboard has been placed contrary to Article 2.1, the game continues but the position reached must be transferred to a correctly placed chessboard.

7.2. If a game has begun with colors reversed then it shall continue, unless the arbiter rules otherwise.

7.3. If a player displaces one or more pieces, that player shall re-establish the correct position while the player's clock is running. If necessary the opponent has the right to restart the player's clock without making a move in order to make sure the player re-establishes the correct position on his or her own time.

7.4. If during a game it is found that an illegal move has been made, or that pieces have been displaced from their squares, the position before the irregularity shall be re-instated. If the position immediately before the irregularity cannot be identified, the game shall continue from the last identifiable position prior to the irregularity. The clocks shall be adjusted according to Article 6.13 and, in the case of an illegal move, Article 4.3 applies to the move replacing the illegal move. The game shall then continue.

Article 8: The Recording of the Moves

8.1. In the course of play each player is required to record all moves by both players, move after move, as clearly and legibly as possible, in the algebraic notation (Appendix E), on the scoresheet prescribed for the competition.

A player may reply to the opponent's move before recording it, but must record that move before making a reply to the opponent's next move.. The offer of a draw must be recorded on the scoresheet by both players.(Appendix E.12) If a player due to physical or religious reasons, is unable to keep score, an amount of time, decided by the arbiter, shall be deducted from the allotted time at the beginning of the game, and an assistant may be supplied to record the game.

8.2. The entire scoresheet shall be made available to the arbiter at any time.

8.3. The scoresheets are the exclusive property of the organizers of the event.

8.4. If a player has less than five minutes left on the clock and does not have additional time of 30 seconds or more added with each move, then the player is not obliged to meet the requirements of Article 8.1. Immediately after one side's time has expired the player must update the scoresheet completely.

8.5. (a) If neither player is required to keep score under Article 8.4, the arbiter or an assistant should attempt to keep score. In this case, immediately after one flag has fallen, the arbiter shall stop the clocks. Then both players shall update their scoresheets, using the arbiter's or the opponent's scoresheet.

(b) If only one player is not required to keep score under Article 8.4, that player must update the scoresheet completely as soon as time has expired in any given time control. Provided it is the player's move, access to opponent's scoresheet is permitted upon request. The player is not permitted to move until after he has completed the scoresheet and returned the opponent's, if it was consulted.

(c) If no complete scoresheet is available, the players must reconstruct the game on a second chessboard under the control of the arbiter or an assistant, who shall first record the actual game position before reconstruction takes place. Notation recorded by demonstration devices may be used to help with the reconstruction.

8.6. If the scoresheets cannot be brought up to date showing that a player has overstepped the allotted time, the next move made shall be considered as the first of the following time period, unless there is evidence that more moves have been made.

Article 9: The Drawn Game

9.1. A player can propose a draw after making a move on the chessboard. This must be done before stopping the clock and starting the opponent's clock. An offer at any other time during play is still valid, but Article 12.5 must be considered. No conditions can be attached to the offer. In both cases the offer cannot be withdrawn and remains valid until the opponent accepts it, rejects it orally, rejects it by making a move, or the game is concluded in some other way.

The offer may be made either orally or by means of a device (see 9.7). Oral offers may be made by any reasonable means which clearly indicate the offer, for example:

[i] "I offer you a draw"
[ii] "Would you like a draw?"
[iii] "Draw?"
[iv] "Remis?" (pronounced Ray-mee)
[v] "Nichya?" (pronounced Nee-chya)

The offer of a draw shall be noted by each player on the scoresheet with the symbol (=).

9.2. The game is drawn, upon a correct claim by the player having the move, when the same position, for at least the third time (not necessarily by repetition of moves)...

(a) is about to appear, if the player first writes the move on the scoresheet and declares to the arbiter the intention to make this move.

(b) has just appeared.

Positions as in (a) and (b) are considered the same, if the same player has the move, pieces of the same kind and color occupy the same squares, and the possible moves of all the pieces of both players are the same. Positions are not the same if a pawn could have been captured en passant or if the right to castle immediately or in the future has been changed.

9.3. The game is drawn, upon a correct claim by the player having the move, if

(a) the player writes on the scoresheet, and declares to the arbiter the intention to make a move which shall result in the last 50 moves having been made by each player without the movement of any pawn and without the capture of any piece, or

(b) the last 50 consecutive moves have been made by each player without the movement of any pawn and without the capture of any piece.

9.4. If the player makes a move without having claimed the draw, the right to claim a draw on that move per Article 9.2 or 9.3, is lost.

9.5. If a player claims a draw as in Article 9.2 or 9.3 the player shall immediately stop both clocks. The player is not allowed to withdraw the claim.

(a) If the claim is found to be correct the game is immediately drawn.

(b) If the claim is found to be incorrect, the arbiter shall deduct half of the claimant's remaining time up to a maximum of three minutes and add three minutes to the opponent's remaining time. Then the game shall continue and the intended move must be made.

9.6. The game is drawn when a position is reached from which a checkmate cannot occur by any possible series of legal moves, even with the most unskilled play (except as per article 10, where applicable). This immediately ends the game.

9.7 A *draw flag* may be used to offer a draw. A draw flag is a device which, when is activated by a player, raises a physical flag or makes visible in some way the offer of the draw to players and arbiters. The organizers may require the use of a draw flag in addition to or in place of the oral offer of a draw.

Article 10: Sudden Death Finish

10.1. A *Sudden Death* finish is the last phase of a game, when all the remaining moves must be made in a limited time with no time increment.

10.2. If the player has less than two minutes left on the clock, the player may claim a draw before the expiration of time by stopping the clocks and summon the arbiter.

(a) If the arbiter is satisfied the opponent is making no effort to win the game by normal means, or that it is not possible to win by normal means, then he shall declare the game drawn. Otherwise he shall postpone the decision.

(b) If the arbiter postpones the decision, the opponent may be awarded two extra minutes thinking time and the game shall continue in the presence of the arbiter.

(c) Having postponed the decision, the arbiter may subsequently declare the game drawn, even after time has expired on one player's clock.

10.3. Illegal moves do not necessarily lose. After the action taken under Article 7.4, for a first illegal move by a player, the arbiter shall give two minutes extra time to the opponent; for a second illegal move by the same player, the arbiter shall give another two minutes extra time to the opponent; for a third illegal move by the same player, the arbiter shall declare the game lost by the player who played incorrectly.

10.4. If the clock shows that time has expired for both players and it is impossible to establish which flag fell first, the game is drawn.

Article 11: Scoring

11.1. A player who wins the game scores one point (1), a player who loses the game scores no points (0) and a player who draws the game scores a half point (1/2).

Article 12: The Conduct of the Players

12.1. High standards of etiquette are expected of the players.

12.2. During play the players are forbidden to make use of any notes, sources of information, advice, or to analyze on another chessboard. The scoresheet shall be used only for recording the moves, the times of the clocks, the offer of a draw, and matters relating to a claim.

12.3. No analysis is permitted in the playing room when play is in progress, whether by players or spectators.

12.4. The players are not allowed to leave the *competition area* without permission from the arbiter. The competition area is defined as the playing area, rest rooms, refreshment area, area set aside for smoking and other places as designated by the arbiter. The player having the move is not allowed to leave the playing area without permission of the arbiter.

12.5. It is forbidden to distract or annoy the opponent in any manner whatsoever; this includes the persistent offer of a draw.

12.6. Infraction of any part of the Articles 12.2 to 12.5 shall lead to penalties in accordance with Article 13.4.

12.7. The game is lost by a player who persistently refuses to comply with the Rules of Chess. The opponent's score shall be decided by the arbiter.

12.8. If both players are found guilty according to Article 12.7, the game shall be declared lost by both players.

Article 13: The Role of the Arbiter

13.1. The arbiter shall see that the Rules of Chess are strictly observed.

13.2. The arbiter shall act in the best interest of the competition. The arbiter should ensure that a good playing environment is maintained and that the players are not disturbed.

13.3. The arbiter shall observe the games, especially when the players are short of time, enforce decisions he has made and impose penalties on players where appropriate.

13.4. Penalties open to the arbiter include:

(a) A warning.

(b) Increasing the remaining time of the opponent.

(c) Reducing the remaining time of the offending player.

(d) Declaring the game to be lost.

(e) Expulsion from the event.

13.5. The arbiter may award either or both players additional time in the event of external disturbance of the game.

13.6. The arbiter must not intervene in a game to indicate the number of moves made, except in applying Article 8.5, when at least one player has used all the allotted time. The arbiter shall refrain from informing a player that the opponent has made a move, or that he has failed to press the clock. The arbiter intervenes after one player's time has expired to require updating of scoresheets, if necessary.

13.7. Spectators and players in other games are not to speak about or otherwise interfere in a game. If necessary, the arbiter may expel offenders from the playing room.

13.8. The ruling of the arbiter may be appealed after the game has concluded by making a written request to the tournament director before the start of the following round, but not later than 2 hours following the conclusion of the game. A deposit may be required by the tournament director. If the ruling of the arbiter is upheld, the deposit may be forfeited in the case that the appeals committee decides that the appeal did not have sufficient basis. If the ruling of the arbiter is modified in any way, the deposit shall be returned promptly.

Article 14: The Role of the Tournament Director

14.1. The tournament director is responsible for all pairings and organizational matters not explicitly belonging to the arbiter.

14.2 The tournament director is responsible for insuring proper lighting and conditions in the playing area, access to refreshments, rest room facilities and displays of information pertaining to the event.

CHESS NOTATION

This section of the rules provides a technical description of the chess notation system as required during play.

E1. Each piece is indicated by an abbreviation. English language values are:

King	K
Queen	Q
Rook	R
Bishop	B
Knight	N
Pawns	(omitted)

E2. Players are free to use the first letter of the name which is commonly used in their own country. In printed matter, iconic representations of the pieces are often used instead of letters, but drawings of pieces may not be used by players when notating a game.

E3. Pawns are not indicated by their first letter, but are recognized by the absence of such a letter.

E4. The eight files (from left to right for White and from right to left for Black) are indicated by the letters, a, b, c, d, e, f, g and h, respectively. Lower case is preferred.

E5. The eight ranks (from bottom to top for White and from top to bottom for Black) are numbered 1, 2, 3, 4, 5, 6, 7 and 8, respectively. In the initial position the white pieces and pawns are placed on the first and second ranks; the black pieces and pawns on the eighth and seventh ranks.

E6. Each of the sixty four squares is therefore indicated by a unique combination of a letter and a number.

E7. Each move of a piece is indicated by (a) the first letter of the name of the piece in question and (b) the square of arrival. There is no hyphen between (a) and (b).

E8. When a piece makes a capture, an x is inserted between the first letter of the name of the piece in question and the square of arrival. When a pawn makes a capture, not only the square of arrival but also the file of departure must be indicated, followed by an x. In the case of an "en passant" capture, the square of arrival is given as the square on which the capturing pawn finally rests.

E9. If two identical pieces can move to the same square, the piece that is moved is indicated as follows:

(1) If both pieces are on the same rank: by the first letter of the name of the piece, the rank of the square of departure, and the square of arrival.

(2) If both pieces are on the same file: by the first letter of the name of the piece, the rank of the square of departure, and the square of arrival.

(3) If the pieces are on different ranks and files, method (1) is preferred. In the case of capture, an x must be inserted before the square of arrival.

E10. If two pawns can capture the same piece or pawn of the opponent, the pawn that is moved is indicated by the letter of the file of departure, an x, the square of arrival

E11. Special moves

In the case of a pawn promotion, the actual pawn move is indicated, followed immediately by the first letter of the new piece. En passant captures require no special indication.

Kingside castling is indicated by two zeroes separated by a dash: 0-0. Queenside castling is represented by three zeroes separated by dashes: 0-0-0.

Check is indicated by a plus sign (+). Checkmate is indicated by the symbol #.

E12. The offer of a draw is indicated by an equal sign (=).

CHESS EQUIPMENT
Chess Sets and Boards

The preferred chess set has the following specifications:

A board with squares 5 cm. x 5 cm. For scholastic events, coordinates (a-h, 1-8) should be imprinted on the edges of the board.

The pawn should have a base with a width equal to one half the size of the square. Four pawns should fit in the area of one square. Lying on its side diagonally on a square, the height of the rook should be equal to the diagonal of the square.

The size of the bishop and knight vary from equal to the height of the rook, to a sharply ascending height. The king is the tallest piece, though the queen may be quite close in height.

The shape of the pieces should correspond to the Staunton design:

In tournaments where players supply their own equipment, the arbiter decides which of the chess sets is closer in design to the preferred set described above.

Chess Clocks

A chess clock is a timing device which has two timers, one for each player, arranged in such a way that if one player's clock is in motion, the other is not. It is typically a digital device (analog clocks are rapidly disappearing and cannot be used for many modern time controls) which can be programmed by the user in a wide variety of ways to impose time limits on the game. Whatever time control is used, the clock should stop in the event that a player exceeds the time limit and some method of indicating the expiration, such as flashing the digits, signals to players, arbiters and spectators that the time has expired.

The Scoresheet

The scoresheet is an important part of tournament play. The large chess databases of tournament games grow because the recording of games is obligatory at chess tournaments. When the organizers provide scoresheets, these are considered property of the tournament. The scoresheet, which is often customized for a major tournament, especially if sponsored, allows the player to record the following:

> The name of the tournament.
> Date of the game.
> Round of the tournament.
> Board number assigned to the game.
> Name of each player.
> Optionally, the rating and team of each player.
> All the moves of the game.
> Optionally, the time for each move.

See the following page for a sample scoresheet.

SAMPLE SCORESHEET

The scoresheet above is from the 5th game of the 2000 Braingames.net World Championship. This is Kasparov's copy. The notation is in Russian, but the moves are easy to follow if you just pay attention to the squares. Kasparov, like many top players, records the clock times on the scoresheet. Notice that move 4 is circled, which seems to be Kasparov's way of indicating that he spent quite a bit of time on his 4th move. Although you can only see hints of it in this example, most players handwriting deteriorates as the game goes on, and when time pressure sets in, things can be almost illegible. Some Grandmasters have totally illegible scoresheets, but an arbiter cannot penalize a player for bad handwriting!

III. RULES FOR SCHOLASTIC CHESS

This section sets forth the special scholastic rules of the Chess Education Association (CEA). These rules were prepared by Richard Peterson, founder of the CEA, in conjunction with many of the CEA chess coaches.

RULE MODIFICATIONS FOR SCHOLASTIC CHESS

In general, CEA has adopted a model that is closer to the world standard, rather than those rules that have been used in the United States. However, the CEA has modified those rules because of the involvement of young and often inexperienced children.

Scholastic chess is unique. While it may be a titanic battle over sixty four squares for an important national championship between professionals, it is more likely to be a learning experience for children and this must be taken into account. The rules must be helpful to the beginner and our young experts who aspire to professional status. It is recognized that circumstances of scholastic events sometimes require modifications of some rules or regulations.

The Chess Education Association delegates to the tournament director and/or arbiter the right to make such adjustments as are necessary for the smooth operation of their events.

However, it is important to remember that using multiple sets of rules only creates confusion in the minds of the players, and that young players in particular, may find themselves applying the wrong roles in a given competition. Therefore, any adjustments to the rules or regulations should be made as minimal as possible. In addition, it is essential that all players, staff, coaches, parents, and other relevant parties, be notified clearly, in writing, of any differences between the official rules and those in effect in a tournament. Below are some examples of rules which are often used to help the scholastic tournament run more smoothly.

- The 50 move rule is not in effect
- First violation of a rule is punished by a warning, rather than the imposition of a penalty

- In the event that the playing venue is about to close, games may be adjudicated with the result determined by the Arbiter
- Players who are not able to record chess notation may instead indicate each move with a checkmark or "x".

THE ROLE OF THE ARBITER IN SCHOLASTIC COMPETITION

Arbiters may take a more active role in scholastic play than in professional competition. They may intervene not only to note a time forfeit or illegal move, but also to correct incorrect board positions at the start of game, to clarify rules whenever the child seems confused, and especially to declare games drawn when they reach technically drawn positions, such as king and knight against king. Arbiters may help to correct scoresheets, since the players' scoresheets are irrelevant to claims of time forfeit and draws. In a scholastic event, the role of the arbiter is not only to enforce the rules, but to provide assistance with understanding the game and letting the players concentrate on their moves.

IV. RULES FOR AMATEUR CHESS

In amateur competition, where no significant prizes are at stake, the standard rules should nevertheless apply. It is important to get used to playing chess properly. Still, in friendly competition some rules may be relaxed.

AMATEUR TOURNAMENTS

The single most important rule for amateur tournaments is that any deviation between the standard rules and the rules of the particular competition be clearly indicated to the participants, preferably in writing. In the United States, it is strongly recommended that differences between the competition rules and those of the United States Chess Federation also be indicated. Organizers of local events often have some very creative ideas about rules, and even more creative ways of justifying them. There really are no restrictions on what an organizer can do, save those imposed by sanctioning bodies, if any. It is the responsibility of the organizer to make modifications clearly understood, but it is the responsibility of the player to follow the rules, no matter how original they may be.

CASUAL PLAY

In games played just for fun, the following modifications are acceptable. Players should make sure that they agree to the terms before the game begins, however, as otherwise disputes are likely to arise.

- Chess clocks need not be used
- The players do not have to keep score
- The draw by three-fold repetition rule need not be enforced
- The fifty-move rule need not be enforced
- The touch move rule need not be enforced.

V. RULES FOR ONLINE CHESS

This section describes the difference between the rules for face-to-face competitions and games played over the Internet.

Software takes many responsibilities away from the player:
- The moves of the game are recorded by the software, so players do not have to keep score.
- The software operates the chess clock automatically
- Technical draws, including three-fold repetition, 50-move rule, and minimum rating material are all automatically enforced
- Illegal moves are not permitted by the software

Unless the competition involves Advanced Chess (where each player is allowed to use a computer analyst while playing), consulting chess playing programs is strictly forbidden. Modern technology allows the Internet Chess Club (ICC) to monitor for use of analysis software running on the same computer, but this remains in large part an ethical question. The ICC allows use of computer analysis only if the player is designated as a "computer-player," indicated online by appending a (C) to the user name.

As for computer databases and opening reference books, the use is governed by the specific rules of the competition. Many players use online games to test out opening ideas, and make free use of notes to do so. Others consider this a heinous crime. As with most amateur competitions, online games should take place in an environment where the rules are clearly stated. If a game is rated, then use of such aids is generally discouraged. If a game is not rated, more relaxed rules may apply, but if you are planning to use notes or databases, you should inform your opponent prior to the start of the game. In the real world, this rarely happens, but there is nothing to prevent you from behaving properly!

Sophisticated technology is used to insure that the time of transmission through the Internet is not deducted from the player's time limit. A timestamp program is built into most user interfaces for online play. The timestamp marks the time actually used by the player.

The Internet Chess Club has the following guidelines regarding some types of behavior that many people consider to be unsporting or rude, related to playing games on ICC. This list is not complete. It just gives examples.

The ICC wants members to be aware that many ICC players may not appreciate these things:
- Using opening books, endgame books, or notes during games. (This is permissible in correspondence games, though).
- When you are lost, letting your time run out instead of resigning.
- Talking to your opponent or kibitzing during the game, unless you know your opponent doesn't mind.
- Offering draws, aborts, or adjourns repeatedly, particularly in dead-lost positions.
- Aborting games on move 1 without reason. Disconnecting before move 5 to get an abort intentionally.
- Kibitzing in other players' games.

They define *abuse* as any action that would give a player a rating that is not "honest," either too high or too low. Such actions include, but are not limited to:
- Intentionally disconnecting in a lost position. Disconnecting in order to analyze the position.
- Refusing to resume an adjourned game when the opponent asks. If you censor or "noplay" someone that you have an adjourned game with, you will probably lose the game by forfeit.
- Intentionally losing games. Resigning games when you are not lost. Accepting multiple wins from a player who is intentionally losing.
- Playing the same player repeatedly during your provisional period in order to get an artificially high rating. Don't play the same player more than 4 rated games during your provisional period (first 20 rated games). Playing most of your games against provisional players during your provisional period is another form of abuse.
- Using a computer without telling the administrators or without putting a note in your finger, or without getting your account added to the computer list. People have the right to know whether they are playing a human or a computer.

- Allowing another person besides you to play rated games with your account. Using another player's account to play rated games. Playing games against yourself on a second account.
- Receiving help from another player or computer while playing a rated game.
- Playing the same line over and over against a computer, to gain rating points. We will edit your rating to whatever we feel is reasonable if you do this.

VI. ETIQUETTE

Chess players everywhere observe some rules of conduct that are traditional courtesies. We shake hands at the start of a game, and shake hands again when it is over (or, if online, send a hello message before the game and a thank you message afterwards). This is the gentlemanly or ladylike way the loser congratulates the winner, and the winner graciously accepts. It never feels good to lose, but we all do so occasionally, and it is rude to display your disappointment by crying or carrying on or any such emotional outburst (unless it is an online game, where the opponent is not subjected to your outburst). Likewise, winning might make you want to burst with joy, but don't celebrate in front of the player you just beat; it's rude.

Another common courtesy is the prohibition against kibitzing (a third party offering advice to one of the players during a game). Such behavior is not only impolite it is also against the rules, which state that chess is a game between two players. The time for analysis or suggestions is after the game is over. As a player there's really not much you can do about kibitzers except to ask them to stop. But you certainly can keep your nose out of other people's games when you are not playing. When observing online games, you may find many players using a "kibitz" function. This is usually the case when the actual game is played offline but is merely being transmitted. Don't worry, the players can't see the information in this case.

In general, it is a good idea to keep silent while chess games are going on. The royal game is not designed to be noisy. A player can speak up during a game is to say "check," but only in amateur games. You cannot say "check" during rated play; it is against the rules. You must speak up when offering a draw, though at some high level competitions an electronic device has been introduced for this purpose.

If a player intends to offer a draw during a timed game, the offer must be made after making a move but before pushing the button on the clock. And if the draw offer is turned down for any reason, don't offer again for a while. Using repeated draw offers to annoy your opponent is both rude and against the rules.

If the opponent has offered a draw in an unrated game and you want to keep playing, simply say so. You technically decline the offer by making a move, but it is better manners to respond in a casual game. Don't try to get cute by being sarcastic. I know of a game where one player had an easily winning position, with several extra queens and a few extra pieces, and thought his opponent should resign, so he sarcastically offered a draw. His opponent naturally accepted, and the tournament director held him to the draw. However, in rated play you should not say anything when declining a draw. Just make your move. A slight shake of the head is considered acceptable.

Never ask your opponent to resign. You win by checkmating your opponent or when he gives up, not before. The best way to encourage a losing player to resign is to play the best moves. The proper way to resign (give up) a game when you see that you're going to get checkmated, is to either say "I resign" or tip your king over. And don't forget to offer your hand.

When should you resign? Beginners are usually advised to never resign. After all, the opponent can always make a mistake! As you get better, you find that opponents will get a bit annoyed if you play on when you have an utterly hopeless position. At more advanced levels, resignation is justified when you are convinced there is no way you can survive, even if your opponent plays very badly, and when all of the spectators would understand why you resigned. The last thing you want to hear when trying to get out the door after a loss is "What happened? Why did you resign?"

There is no reason to resign in an endgame unless you cannot stop your opponent from obtaining an overwhelming advantage, such as a new queen. There are many tricky draws in the endgame, and the endgame is usually a player's weakest area.

When the game is over, it's a good idea to ask your opponent or coach to go over the game with you, particularly if you've lost. That's the best way to find out what mistakes you have made so you can correct them in the future. This analysis is best done in another room, though. One of the most annoying things during a tournament is for nearby players to noisily analyze their game while you're still playing. You will find that tournament directors can get quite testy about this, and many have been known to knock over the pieces or otherwise disrupt the analysis to get the players to leave the room.

We recommend the director simply remove the kings. It should go without saying that when your tournament game is complete you should not start to play blitz. A good arbiter or director will immediately seize the chess clock when this happens.

The French term "j'adoube" (or English equivalent "adjust") is only meant for adjusting a piece or when you inadvertently brushed a piece on the way to moving something else. The touch move rule is always strictly enforced in tournaments, and it is a good idea to get into good habits from the start.

VII. CHESS TOURNAMENTS

Chess tournaments range from modest weekend affairs with trophy prizes to the World Championship competition where the prize fund is millions of dollars! In many professional competitions, the participants have all their expenses paid and receive an "appearance fee" which can be tens of thousands of dollars.

The standard form of tournament is called a Swiss System. There is no elimination. Each round, players are paired with others who share the same score. After the first round, all the winners play another winner, losers are paired with losers, and those whose first game ended in a draw face each other. Weekend tournaments usually have 4-5 rounds. Major national events have 6-7 rounds, and international tournaments are 9-11 rounds. One nice thing about this system is that when you lose, you usual face weaker competition, and it is easy to work your way back into contention.

Sometimes tournaments involve an odd number of players, in which case one player must sit out (though some tournaments provide "house players" to avoid this problem). In this case, the player receives a full point as compensation. This is known as getting a *bye*. The bye goes to the player who occupies the lowest position in the standings, but no player may receive more than one bye. In some American tournaments, players can receive a *half-point bye* on request. Without playing the game, they receive the same result as if they had drawn the game!

Some of these tournaments allow multiple half-point byes without affecting eligibility for prizes. This sort of nonsense is confined, thankfully, to American tournaments. The justification for this is that it allows players with busy schedules to compete in tournaments, but in reality that is only a way of saying that organizers can take in more entry fees. In some sanctioned USCF tournaments, a player can even buy a re-entry to the event, and take half-point byes for the rounds missed.

Some competitions are designed to pack as much chess as possible into a short period of time, while others have a leisurely pace, so that players can do some sightseeing and relax. Most American tournaments are of the first type, with a few exceptions, such as the Hawaii International Chess Festival. Europe and the rest of the world tend to prefer the second type. Often tournaments are held in resorts, for example along the Spanish coast of the Mediterranean, the Balearic Islands, the Canary Islands, Isle of Man, Cannes and Hungary's Lake Balaton. Chess tournaments are held in virtually every major city in the world. In America, the biggest tournaments are held in Las Vegas, Los Angeles, New York and Philadelphia.

Entry fees range from about $10 to $250, usually depending on how much money can be won. Most require membership in a national or international chess organization. In most of the world, chess sets, boards and clocks are provided, though in America, players are often required to bring their own equipment. You can find out about American tournaments by visiting the web site of the USCF (www.uschess.org).

For details on organizing competitions, we refer the reader to Stewart Reuben's excellent *Chess Organizers' Handbook*, published by Everyman. We provide some details of tournaments below, but the complex mathematics of the system are beyond the scope of this book.

TYPES OF TOURNAMENTS

There are many different kinds of chess tournaments. some are used in professional competition, but others are only found in casual and amateur play. All of these formats can be used for rated play.

Swiss System

The Swiss System is a system where players are paired according to their results. The precise details of pairing systems are complex, but the basic principle is that in each round a player will be faced with an opponent who was the same number of points. No player may face the same opponent twice, and at the end of the competition players should have, if possible, an equal number of games with the White and Black pieces.

Because the formulas used to pair opponents are quite complicated, pairings are usually made by computers. The Chess Education Association recommends the use of the SwissSys program. However, there are times when a computer pairing program is not available. In this case, the easiest and fairest system is as follows:

1. Divide the players according to their score.
2. For each group, divide the players into three sections according to their due color (White, Black, doesn't matter)
3. Equalize score groups so that half the players will be assigned White, half will be assigned Black
4. Pair the top half of the White group against the bottom half of the Black group, and vice versa

Disputes about pairings are very common. Players often complain that an error has been made, even when pairings are made by computer. Many times the protests evaporate when it becomes clear that the protester failed to take into account some small piece of data.

The late Norwegian organizer Arnold Eikrem had a great system for dealing with such protests. He simply handed the pairing cards (used in pre-computer days, but even now the computers can print them on demand) to the protester and asked the protester to go away, determine the "proper" pairings and then he would take a look. To his credit, on the rare occasions the protest was justified, he corrected the pairings immediately.

It must be pointed out that in American tournaments, the tournament director often posts the pairings immediately before the start of the round, and then when confronted by errors, exclaims that it is too late to make changes. Of course pairings should be posted as soon as they are ready, and a bit of time should be reserved to take into account problems that arise. In the section on the role of the tournament director, we present a method of making rapid corrections when pairings are incorrect.

Round Robin Tournaments

The round robin system has been used in most classical chess competitions and is considered the fairest system of all. Each player plays each other player in one (*single round robin*) or two (*double round robin*) games. At the end of the competition, all players were ranked with ties broken according to various systems, which are described in the tie-break section.

Round Robin System		
Name	**Number of Players**	**# games by Player**
Quad	4	3
Double Quad	4	6
Hexagonal	6	5
Double Hex	6	10
Octagon	8	7
Double Octagon	8	14

You can find pairing charts for many different numbers of players in the appendix.

Matches

The simplest form of competition is a one-on-one match of between 6 to 24 games. Matches have an even number of games so that the distribution of games with Black and White even out. The winner is the player with the most points, or the first player to win a specified number of games.

Team Matches

In their team match, each member of each team plays one member of the opposing team one or two games. Prior to the start of the competition, the teams present each other with a list players in order of ranking. The top player on one team plays against the top player on the other team, the second best player faces the opposing second best player, and so on until all players are matched up.

Scheveningen System

The Scheveningen System is a form of competition where each member of each team plays against each member of the opposing team. Scheveningen tournaments are appropriate for teams of four to twelve players. (Pairing charts are provided on page 84.)

Schiller System

The Schiller system can be used for team or individual competitions. It combines aspects of the Round Robin and Scheveningen

Systems. Each player faces all of the other players except those on the same team. It works best with an even number of teams, since otherwise one team will have to sit out each round, though that is an option for league play.

Schiller System			
Players	*Teams*	*Players per team*	*Total Games*
8	4	2	6
12	4	3	9
12	6	2	10
16	4	4	12
16	8	2	14
20	4	5	15
20	10	2	18
24	4	6	18
24	6	4	20
24	8	3	21
24	12	2	22

Pairings are made according to the charts in Appendix A.

Knockout Format

The knockout format is used for an elimination event. This format has the advantage of producing a clear winner for every tournament, and the disadvantage that those players who are eliminated do not gain the experience or pleasure of additional games. It is best used when there are 8, 16, 32, 64, or 128 participants. Normally, ties are resolved by additional games (often played at a faster time control). These playoff games are generally two game matches, so that the advantage of playing with the White pieces is not excessive.

Double Knockout

A double knockout format allows players who have lost to be placed into a "rebound" section with players who lost in previous rounds. It takes two losses to be eliminated from competition.

Ladders

Chess clubs often make use of the ladder system, where players are initially ordered according to their ratings, and then may challenge players higher on the list. Rules and regulations vary from club to club. The main appeal of a ladder system is that players can play whenever they want and can accept or declining challenges as they choose.

TIE-BREAKING METHODS

In all of the systems discussed above, with the exception of knock down and ladder tournaments, players may have equal standing at the end of the competition. In this case, some sort of tie-breaking method is usually used to determine winners of trophies and non-cash prizes. No tie-breaking method is fair to all participants, and each involves compromise. The best way of resolving ties is to use playoffs, even if these require games to be played at a faster time limit. However, the following alternatives are available.

Performance Rating

Using performance ratings to break ties is perhaps the fairest method, and it is one of the easiest to calculate. The ratings of each player's opponents are averaged, and the performance rating can be calculated by the formula: Rating Average + 400 x wins-losses/number of games. So, if a player faces an average opposition of 1600, and scores 8 points from 10, then the performance rating is 1600+ (2400/10) = 1840. This can be used for all forms of competition, but is not well-suited to Round Robin events because the only difference between tied players will be their initial rating.

Bucholtz

The Bucholtz system awards the tie-break by adding together the scores earned by each player's opponents. This is the most frequently applied system, though it is not very accurate in placing players properly. Each player receives the full score of each defeated opponent, with half the score awarded in case of a draw (or tied match). For example, in a ten round event each opponent will have a final score of between zero and 10 points, so that a possible 100 points can be accumulated. A common variation is to exclude the result of the lowest-scoring opponent.

Color-Adjusted Score

Stewart Reuben recommends giving a bonus to players who have had the Black pieces in more games. This eminently fair proposal has not been used, as far as we know, but one method is to adjust the score as follows: deduct .1 for each game where the player had White, add .1 for each game where the player had Black, and make no adjustment if the game was unplayed (a forfeit or bye).

Progressive Score

Progressive score is calculated by adding up the score a player has after each round of competition. This method has little to recommend itself except for ease of calculation, and should not be used for serious events. A loss in an early round can doom a player from the start.

WITHDRAWING FROM A TOURNAMENT

In most of the world, entrance into a tournament represents a commitment to play all the games scheduled. Even if a player is doing badly, there is a moral obligation to stick it out and fight to the end. In American tournaments, however, players often withdraw from a tournament for a variety of reasons, including a poor performance or simply a desire to get home early if a prize is not likely. Such withdrawals have an effect on the rest of the players, and may change the prize distribution by affecting tie-breaks.

Withdrawals in many American tournaments are not penalized provided that the tournament director has been notified in a timely fashion, preferably before pairings are made for the next round. In some tournaments, such as the Hawaii Internationals, withdrawal is only possible with the permission of the tournament director.

HOW TO READ CROSSTABLES AND REPORTS

At any tournament, there is a variety of information provided to participants and spectators during the course of the event. In addition to the pairing charts shown above, there are presentations of crosstables, standings, rating reports and individual round results. In this section we provide some samples and explain how they should be interpreted.

Crosstables

The *crosstable* is the document which shows the results of the tournament, updated each round. It includes a ranking, player name, rating at the start of the event and the opponent, color and result for each game played. It may also contain an indication of the federation of the player, international title, performance rating and tie-breaks. The following is a crosstable from a master event, incorporating the title into the player name and omitting non-essential fields for the sake of clarity. The followng page explains the information.

Frisco Masters International
Mechanics' Institute, San Francisco USA
March 31-April 3rd 2000

#	Name	Rtng	Rd 1	Rd 2	Rd 3	Rd 4	Rd 5	Rd 6	Rd 7	Total
1	GM Ehlvest, Jaan	2709	W18	W8	L3	D24	W14	W16	W7	5.5
2	GM Yermolinsky, Alex	2693	W19	W16	D12	D4	D3	W11	W8	5.5
3	GM Shabalov, Alex	2623	W20	W13	W1	W5	D2	D8	D4	5.5
4	GM Fedorowicz, John	2616	W26	W33	H—	D2	D5	W10	D3	5.0
5	IM Ziatdinov, Rashid	2536	W29	W35	W15	L3	D4	D6	W13	5.0
6	Longren, William	2297	L15	D25	W32	W40	W28	D5	W12	5.0
7	GM Browne, Walter	2541	D21	W30	W24	D12	W24	H—	L1	4.5
8	IM Barcenilla, Rogelio	2458	W27	L1	W26	W37	W12	D3	L2	4.5
9	Small, Gregg	2347	H—	B—	L24	L21	W38	W34	W19	4.5
10	Evans, Bela	2295	D28	L24	W27	W25	W20	L4	W16	4.5
11	Acosta, Mariano	2200	W17	H—	L19	W36	W21	L2	W25	4.5
12	GM Blatny, Pavel	2614	W42	W37	D2	D7	L8	W14	L6	4.0
13	IM Ivanov, Igor	2423	W38	L3	L37	W26	W29	W17	L5	4.0
14	IM Rey, Guillermo	2421	D32	W22	W28	H—	L1	L12	W26	4.0
15	IM Cela, Altin	2604	W6	D34	L5	L20	D18	H—	W30	3.5
16	IM Ilic, Zoran	2465	W31	L2	W11	W19	H—	L1	L10	3.5
17	Iskhanov, Tigran	2335	L11	L29	W41	W33	W37	L13	D20	3.5
18	Lobo, Richard	2335	L1	D27	W30	L28	D15	W21	D22	3.5
19	Pruess, David	2314	L2	W31	W33	L16	W35	H—	L9	3.5
20	Stearns, Aaron	2312	L3	H—	W22	W15	L10	D25	D17	3.5
21	Ilfeld, Etan	2289	D7	L23	W39	W9	L11	L18	W31	3.5
22	Wong, Russell	2205	D40	L14	L20	B—	H—	W29	D18	3.5
23	IM McCambridge, V.	2511	D30	W21	H—	D34	U—	U—	D27	3.0
24	Bhat, Vinay	2427	H—	W10	W9	D1	L7	U—	U—	3.0
25	Martinez, Marcel	2418	L33	D6	W35	L10	W32	D20	L11	3.0
26	WIM Reizniece, Dana	2309	L4	W38	L8	L13	W39	W37	L14	3.0
27	Braden, Arthur	2258	L8	D18	L10	L39	B—	W38	D23	3.0
28	Mezentsev, Vladimir	2558	D10	W32	L14	W18	L6	U—	U—	2.5
29	Poehlmann, Roger	2287	L5	W17	D36	H—	L13	L22	D33	2.5
30	Pupols Viktors	2282	D23	L7	L18	L35	W33	W39	L15	2.5
31	Shakhnazarov, Oleg	2259	L16	L19	D38	L32	W41	W35	L21	2.5
32	Schiller, Eric	2220	D14	L28	L6	W31	L25	H—	D35	2.5
33	Lazetich, Zoran	2219	W25	L4	L19	L17	L30	B—	D29	2.5
34	Pinto, Mark	2203	B—	D15	H—	D23	U—	L9	U—	2.5
35	Blohm, David	2200	B—	L5	L25	W30	L19	L31	D32	2.5
36	Van Buskirk, Charles	2424	L37	W41	D29	L11	H—	U—	U—	2.0
37	Haessler, Carl	2251	W36	L12	W13	L8	L17	L26	U—	2.0
38	Harmon, Clark	2244	L13	L26	D31	W41	L9	L27	D39	2.0
39	Hernandez, Rodolfo	2200	H—	L40	L21	W27	L26	L30	D38	2.0
40	Baja, Victor	2394	D22	W39	L7	L6	U—	U—	U—	1.5
41	Levin, Eugene	2200	H—	L36	L17	L38	L31	U—	U—	0.5
42	IM Shipman, Walter	2299	L12	U—	U—	U—	U—	U—	U—	0.0

THE OFFICIAL RULES OF CHESS • CARDOZA PUBLISHING

Explanation of the Preceding Chart

The first column contains the current rank of the player in the event.

The second column contains the name of the player preceded by an international title if any. The official international playing titles of FIDE, the world chess federation, are:

Abbreviation	Title
GM	International Grandmaster
IM	International Master
FM	FIDE Master
WGM	Woman Grandmaster
WIM	Woman International Master
WFM	Woman FIDE Master

In addition, you will sometimes see NM for National Master.

The third column contains the rating for each player at the start of the tournament. If a player has no rating, there may be a zero, "unrated" or nothing at all. The next 7 columns contain the results of each game for the 7-round event. The result contains a letter indicating the result and a number indicating the final rank of the opponent in the tournament or when there was no opponent. Often the color will be indicated by putting the letter in boldface to indicate the player had White (or Black, there isn't a great deal of consistency among formats). Finally, the total score earned by the players is given. Sometimes tie-break information is added.

W= Win, L= Loss, D=Draw, H= Half-point bye, X= Full point bye or forfeit win, U= unplayed

---

The results of a round-robin tournament are usually presented in a crosstable like the one below.

Arthur Dake International Rating Tournament
Mechanics' Institute, San Francisco

					1	2	3	4	5	6	7	8	9	10
1	Baker, J.	USA	2194	7	•	1	1/2	1	0	1	1	1/2	1	1
2	Schiller, E.	USA	2209	6	0	•	1	1/2	1	1	0	1	1/2	1
3	Wong, R.	USA	2021	5	1/2	0	•	1/2	0	0	1	1	1	1
4	Grey, P.	USA		5	0	1/2	1/2	•	1/2	1	1/2	1	1	0
5	Margulis, I.	USA	2295	5	1	0	1	1/2	•	0	1	0	1/2	1
6	Pinto, M.	USA	2154	5	0	0	1	0	1	•	1/2	1/2	1	1
7	Aigner, M.	USA		4	0	1	0	1/2	0	1/2	•	1	0	1
8	Steel, D.	USA	2058	3.5	1/2	0	0	0	1	1/2	0	•	1	1/2
9	Stevens, P.	USA		2.5	0	1/2	0	0	1/2	0	1	0	•	1/2
10	Bambou, C.	FRA		2	0	0	0	1	0	0	0	1/2	1/2	•

The players are listed in order of final result, or in the order of the pairing numbers assigned at the start of the tournament. In the past, the latter was the case as computers were not available to rearrange the results. Computer programs now process the information so that the order of finish presentation is the most common. The result of

45

each game can be presented in several different ways. In this case, a win is indicated by "1", a draw by "1/2" and a loss by "0". Sometimes "+", "=", and "–" are used, or "W", "D", and "L".

Standings

The standings are usually presented with ratings and tie-break information. In the chart below, produced by Swiss Perfect, both International (Rtg) and local (Loc) ratings are supplied for each player, and three tie-breaks (Median Bucholtz, Bucholtz and Progressive) are provided.

Pl	Name	Feder	Rtg	Loc	Score	M-Buch.	Buch.	Progr.
1	Baker, Jonathan	USA	2194	2267	7	30.0	38.0	34.5
2	Schiller, Eric	USA	2209	2217	6	30.0	39.0	30.0
3-6	Wong, Russell	USA	2021	2237	5	31.0	40.0	30.5
	Grey, Peter	USA	2034		5	31.0	40.0	29.0
	Margulis, Isaak	USA	2295	2278	5	31.0	40.0	27.5
	Pinto, Mark	USA	2154	2200	5	31.0	40.0	22.5
7	Aigner, Michael	USA	2117		4	32.0	41.0	17.5
8	Steel, David	USA	2058	1976	3.5	32.5	41.5	14.0
9	Stevens, Peter	USA	2052		2.5	33.5	42.5	11.5
10	Bambou, Christophe	FRA	1894		2 3	3.5	43.0	8.0

Rating Reports

A *rating report* shows a player's rating at the start of the event (Rtg), the score achieved with number of games, the score expected of a player with the indicated rating, the change in rating, and finally the performance rating of the player. In the example provided, from the same tournament as above, you can see that Baker and Wong did much better than expected and gained points, while Margulis lost points and the ratings of Schiller, Pinto and Steel were not greatly affected.

No	Name	Rtg	Score	Exp.	Change	Rprfm
1.	Baker, Jonathan	2194	7.0/9	5.85	12	2305
2.	Schiller, Eric	2209	6.0/9	6.03	0	2208
3.	Pinto, Mark	2154	5.0/9	5.31	-3	2133
4.	Margulis, Isaak	2295	5.0/9	6.93	-19	2127
5.	Wong, Russell	2021	5.0/9	3.51	15	2147
6.	Steel, David	2058	3.5/9	3.96	-5	2020
7.	Aigner, Michael	*	4.0/9			2053
8.	Stevens, Peter	*	2.5/9			1928
9.	Grey, Peter	*	5.0/9			2139
10.	Bambou, Christophe	*	2.0/9			1868

The last four players had no international ranking prior to the start of play. An international ranking can be earned only with a performance of 2000 or higher, so only Aigner and Grey earned an international rating, while Stevens and Bambou must try again at another event.

Results of an Individual Round

The results of individual games in a round are presented with board number, name of White player, result and name of Black player. Here is a sample:

No	Name	Result	Name
1	Wong, Russell	1:0	Bambou, Christophe
2	Steel, David	1:0	Margulis, Isaak
3	Aigner, Michael	.5:.5	Pinto, Mark
4	Stevens, Peter	.5:.5	Schiller, Eric
5	Grey, Peter	0:1	Baker, Jonathan

Additional information is often provided, for example:

The Schuhplatter Chess Tournament
9th Veterans vs Ladies
Munich, Germany, July 4th-15th 2000.
Round 1 (July 4, 2000) Ladies 3.5 - Veterans 1.5

Galliamova-Ivanchuk, Alisa	- Smyslov, Vassily	1/2	34	D12	Slav defence
Ioseliani, Nana	- Korchnoi, Viktor	1/2	39	E41	Nimzo-indian
Polgar, Sofia	- Hort, Vlastimil	1-0	32	B33	Sicilian:Sveshnikov
Xie Jun	- Bouwmeester, Hans	1/2	38	C54	Italian Game
Zhu Chen	- Taimanov, Mark	1-0	40	E11	Bogo-indian

The White player is listed first, followed by the Black player. The result is then given, where 1-0 indicates a White win, 0-1 marks a Black win, and 1/2 is used for a draw. The next column shows how many moves were played in the game. The next item, a letter followed by a two-digit number, refers to the opening code used in the *Encyclopedia of Chess Openings*. This is known as the ECO code. The last column contains the name of the opening.

RECOMMENDED PRIZE DISTRIBUTION

Prizes for chess competitions include money, trophies, plaques, medals, books and chess equipment. Large cash prizes are not recommended for amateur events. One good rule of thumb is that the first prize in an amateur event (or section of a larger tournament) should not exceed the total cost of attending the event, including entrance fees, hotel costs, meals and reasonable travel expenses. For professional events, prizes should be appropriate to the level of competition.

Cash Prizes

Since cash prizes are not generally subject to tie-breaks, it should be kept in mind that many of these prizes will be shared. There are no universally accepted formulas for assigning cash prizes, but in general the first prize should be almost double the second prize, which should be approximately one and a half times as large as the third prize. Assuming five prizes totaling $1200, a good distribution is $500-$300-$200-$100-$100.

A system developed by Czech Grandmaster Vlastimil Hort can also be recommended. In his system, half of the money is divided equally among those tied, with Bucholtz tie-break used to distribute the rest.

Trophies and Other Prizes

Trophies, medals, plaques and other items are commonly awarded at chess competitions, especially in amateur and scholastic events. Additional prizes may be contribute by sponsors, and may include chess books, software, even discount coupons for food and travel. Such prizes create a lasting impression on the winners, and should be strongly encouraged. The organizer must keep in mind that some items are rather awkward to carry. Trophies can be too large to fit into an airline overhead bin, for example. Large trophies are, however, popular with scholastic players.

Section Prizes

If a tournament is held in rating or section groups, then the highest rated/oldest groups should have the highest prizes. Some tournaments, especially in America, have large prizes available to low rated players, offering, for example, $1,000 for the best result by a player rated under 1200. This is basically done to justify high entry fees and encourage low rated players to participate, but there is a dark side: There is a temptation for young and inexperienced players to cheat. It is better to offer trophy and book prizes, or other items, to reward success in the lower-rated groups.

Since prizes are sometimes provided by an outside party, there may be no adequate method of splitting the prize. In such cases, the organizer should provide a competitive over the board method of deciding who the victor shall be.

VIII. TIME CONTROLS

Chess is played with a chess clock to insure that the game will end within some definite period of time. Players who fail to make the required number of moves within the specified period lose the game.

The rules require that each player arrive at the board within 60 minutes of the published starting time of the game. If the posted starting time is, say, five o'clock in the afternoon and the opponent doesn't arrive by six o'clock, the game is forfeited. The latecomer is given no point, while the waiting player records a win. It doesn't matter that the chess clock shows less than an hour remaining.

STANDARD TIME CONTROLS

The modern standard time control is forty moves in two hours by each player, followed by either all remaining moves in an additional hour each, or another 20 moves in the next hour, followed by all remaining moves in thirty minutes.

Things are changing, however, and incremental time controls are increasingly popular. These involve reserving a fixed period of time for each move. In serious chess, this time period is often between ten and thirty seconds per move.

For the Braingames.net World Championship, a time control of 40 moves in two hours followed by 20 moves in one hour followed by all moves in 30 minutes with an additional ten seconds (non-accumulating) per move was used. Actually, this turned out to be an approximation because the digital clock failed to handle this time control correctly.

In some tournaments organized by FIDE, the first time control might be 40 moves in 100 minutes, with an additional 30 seconds per move. That works out to the same control as 40 moves in two hours, except that under all circumstances a player must have at least thirty seconds for each move, where without the increment one can run out of time altogether. The second time control is 20 moves in 50 minutes, again with 30 seconds per move. The final time control can be all moves in 20 minutes, with 30 seconds per move. As we go to press, FIDE is planning to shorten the time control considerably.

AMATEUR TIME CONTROLS

Amateur tournaments are often designed to get as many games as possible into a fixed time period. Often these events are held at schools and other facilities, which have a strict limit on when events must end. It is not uncommon to see three or even four games played in one day. In general, however, amateur tournaments have two games per day. Time controls vary greatly, but some of the more popular ones are all moves in two hours, 30 moves in ninety minutes followed by all moves in an hour, and 45 or 50 moves in two hours.

David Bronstein recommends 15 minutes per player per game for casual chess, and 30 minutes for more "creative" games. In the incremental control, this could be 10 minutes per game with a 5-second increment in the friendly games, and 20 minutes with a 10 second increment for more serious encounters.

Special rules apply in the case of games played at a rapid time control.

R1. A *rapid* game is one where all the moves must be made in a fixed time of not less than 15 minutes and no longer than one hour per player per game.

R2. Play shall be governed by the Rules of Chess, except where they are overridden by the following Rules.

R3. Players are not required to record the moves.

R4. Once each player has made three moves, no claim can be made regarding incorrect piece placement, orientation of the chessboard or clock setting.

R5. The arbiter shall make a ruling according to Articles 4 and 10, only if requested to do so by one or both players.

R6. The time is considered to have expired when a valid claim to that effect has been made by a player. The arbiter shall refrain from signaling the expiration of time.

R7. To claim a win on time, the claimant must stop both clocks and notify the arbiter. For the claim to be successful, the claimant must have time remaining on the clock and the opponent must have no time remaining.

R8. If the clock shows time expired for both players, the game is drawn.

COMMONLY USED TIME CONTROLS

	Classic	Modern
Professional	40 moves in 120 min, then 20 moves in 60 min, then all moves in 30 min	40 moves in 120 min then 20 moves in 60 min then all moves in 30 min, with 10 seconds added each move of this final period.
Master	40 moves in 120 min, then all moves in 60 minutes	40 moves in 120 min, then all moves in 60 min, with 30 seconds added each move
Expert	all moves in 120 min	all moves in 120 min, with 10 seconds added each move
Amateur	30 moves in 90 min, then all moves in 60 min	all moves in 75 min with 10 seconds added each move
Club	all moves in 60 min	all move in 60 minutes with 5 seconds added each move
Sport	all moves in 30 min	all move in 20 minutes with 10 seconds added each move
Rapid	all moves in 15 min	all move in 10 minutes with 10 seconds added each move
Blitz	all moves in 5 min	all moves in 3 min with 5 seconds added each move
Superblitz	all move in 3 min	All moves in 2 min with 2 seconds added each move
Bullet	all moves in 2 min	All moves in 1 min with 1 second added each move
Lightning	10 seconds per move	10 seconds per move
Hourglass	An initial amount of time is specified, and a player loses if the difference between the player's time and the opponent's time exceeds that amount.	An initial amount of time is specified, and a player loses if the difference between the player's time and the opponent's time exceeds that amount.

BLITZ CHESS

Blitz chess, also known as "rapids," is usually played at a rate of five minutes per player per game, sometimes even faster with three-minute chess and "bullet" chess, which allows only one or two seconds per move, especially popular on the internet. Blitz players sometimes use special rules, which are not consistent. The World Blitz Chess Association has not yet had its rules universally adopted. In many cases, the official FIDE rules are used for blitz chess as well.

B1. A *blitz* game is one where all the moves must be made in a fixed time of less than 15 minutes per player per game.

B2. Play shall be governed by the rules for rapid chess except where they are overridden by the following Laws.

B3. An illegal move is completed once the opponent's clock has been started. The opponent is then entitled to claim a win before making a move. Once the opponent has made a move, an illegal move cannot be corrected.

B4. In order to win, a player must have *sufficient mating force*. This is defined as adequate forces to eventually produce a checkmate. Any position where the player has a queen, rook or pawn has sufficient mating force. Any position where the player has two pieces has sufficient mating force, unless both pieces are knights. The only cases of insufficient mating force are:

(a) Bare king,
(b) A single bishop
(c) One or two knights.

B5. Article 10.2 does not apply.

WHAT HAPPENED TO ADJOURNMENTS?

Until recently, most tournaments and matches allowed for adjournments - delaying games until a later time - usually after the first or second time control. Often games were not finished until a second, third, or even fourth day! At first, players were not allowed to consult with other players, analysts or computers but eventually the rules were relaxed. In most of the World Championships, especially after World War II, the combatants employed teams of "seconds" to assist with the analysis of adjourned games.

Modern tournaments do not allow for adjournments, but have had to accelerate the time controls in order to complete the games in a single playing session, usually six or seven hours.

IX. CHESS RATING SYSTEMS

There are many rating and rankings systems in the chess world. All of the most respected ratings use a system developed by Professor Arpad Elo with a few minor modifications. We present a few of the major ranking lists below, each of which uses a scale of approximately zero to 3000. In each case the numbers can be translated to the following descriptive equivalents:

0-500	Absolute beginner
500-1000	Beginner
1000-1300	Intermediate
1300-1600	Club Player
1600-2000	Tournament Player
2000-2200	Candidate Master
2200-2400	Master
2400-2500	International Master
2500-2600	Grandmaster
2600-2700	Elite Grandmaster
2700+	World Class

The common factors of the rating lists involve the premise that a player is given an expected score based on the rating of the player and rating of the opponents, and that the rating is adjusted based on how the player's actual result compares with the expected result. The "k-factor" is a constant used to make the adjustment. Put simply, if, on the basis of the ratings, a player is expected to score 5 points out of ten, but only scores 3, then the player would lose 2 times the k-factor, which can be anywhere from 10 to 25 depending on the system used. If the player scored 7, then the player would gain 2 times the k-factor. If the player scored 5 points, no change would take place. Additional examples are provided in the rating section below.

The individual characteristics of the rating lists are presented below.

PROFESSIONAL CHESS RATINGS

The latest, and most accurate rating system is based on ideas from Ken Thompson, a distinguished guru of computer software who has had a lifelong interest in chess. This system is more complex than the previously developed systems, and it takes into account such important factors as whether a player has White or Black, and how frequently the player competes. Unlike the pure Elo system, the number of points gained by one player and lost by the opponent are not necessarily equal. For a single game one player might gain ten points, while the opponent loses six.

WORLD CHESS FEDERATION RATINGS

The World Chess Federation (FIDE) maintains a standard rating list for both professional and amateur players rated over 2000. This system is based on the original rating list worked out by Professor Arpad Elo. It has lost some credibility due to political suspensions (for example the brief suspensions of Garry Kasparov and Nigel Short after their renegade match in 1993) and wild inflation in some countries (Myanmar was the most notable example). Nevertheless, it remains the most accepted rating list since the professional list is confined to elite players.

UNITED STATES CHESS FEDERATION RATINGS

The USCF has made many little changes to the system developed by Elo, including such concepts as "feedback points," "bonus points," "rating floors" and others. They are presently experimenting with new modifications, which have been called "fiddle points" by some critics. To be fair, the USCF faces a difficult task as they deal with the entire range of rated players, not just experienced players of a particular standard. They must accommodate new players who may quickly improve their skills, and imported players from foreign countries who have already acquired professional skills.

There are also specific problems that arise in isolated communities, including chess played in prisons, where there is very little change in the rating pool, which can maintain a stagnant average rating even while skill levels rise, or which can allow a single player to absorb most of the points in the pool. At one time the USCF ratings were about 80-100 points higher than the international equivalents. However, the mixed bag includes both players with higher US ratings and higher international ratings.

Recent changes to the USCF system are described in the October 2000 issue of *Chess Life* magazine. You can get more information on the USCF system at their website, www.uschess.org.

INTERNET CHESS CLUB RATINGS

The Internet Chess Club offers not one, but up to six different ratings depending on the type of game played. The most important rating is the Standard rating, which measures games played at a rate of more than 15 minutes per game. The second significant rating is the Blitz rating, which applies to games played at a faster rate of play. The other ratings are of no real significance, applying either to non-standard chess or standard chess played at the silly rate of two minutes per game or less, which is really just a test of eye-hand coordination.

CEA RATINGS

The Chess Education Association has its own rating system constructed with scholastic chess in mind. The system is based on the knowledge that young people are capable of great leaps of understanding and thus allows successful young players to leap quickly in the ratings.

In the CEA system, no one is ever unrated. Experienced players will use their existing "foreign" rating. For instance, if a youngster had a USCF or Canadian rating of 1357, CEA will use that rating as the starting point for that player. New players come in with an initial rating based upon their age at the time of their first rated game.

Players under the age of 6 are assigned a rating of 500. Players from 6-10 years of age receive a rating equal to 100 times their age. Players over 10 years of age receive an initial rating of 1000 plus 50 points for each year over 10. Thus, if a player is 15 years old he or she receives a rating of 1000 + (50 x 5) for a rating of 1250.

From the time of their initial entry into the CEA system, ratings will fluctuate up and down with the performance of the players. Each game is worth 25 point, plus or minus 5% of the difference in the player's ratings. However, all games are worth at least one point.

Following are some examples.

Player A	Result	Player B	Rating A	Rating B
1200	Defeats	1200	+25	-25
1200	Defeats	1000	+15	-15
1200	Loses to	1000	-35	+35
1450	Loses to	1050	-45	+45
1450	Defeats	1050	+5	-5

In the CEA system, the number of points gained and the number of points lost should always be the same. The first three examples are straightforward. In the last two, there is a difference of 400 rating points which forces a special rule to apply

In the fourth case, the game is worth 25 points plus there is a four hundred point difference x 5% equals 20 points for a total of 45 points.

In the fifth example, once again the game is worth 25 points minus 5% of the 400-point difference or 20 points. This results in a net gain of 5 points to Player A and a net loss to Player B of 5 points.

This system was designed to give greater flexibility to young players ratings. Since ratings change rapidly, their accuracy should not be over emphasized. CEA ratings should be seen as batting averages, which rise and fall every game, rather than something that is fixed and static. It is not necessary for coaches to learn to calculate the changes in ratings since the calculations are performed by the software, but it is useful to understand the principles presented above.

X. CHESS TEACHERS, COACHES AND TRAINERS

You don't have to be a strong player to enjoy the international world of chess. Most tournaments are either open to all players, or have amateur sections alongside the professional competitions. Of course, knowledge of the rules is essential, and no one want to enter a competition and lose all of their games. In addition to chess books and software, many players turn to teachers, coaches and trainers to improve their game.

A chess teacher usually works only at an elementary level. The instruction includes the rules, basic middlegame and endgame strategy, and perhaps a small opening repertoire. Chess teachers usually work in schools and at special chess camps. A good teacher will be a competitive player, usually rated at least 1700. The instruction will be balanced in all areas of the game, and the openings taught will be standard chess openings.

Many teachers prefer to teach trappy openings designed to bring quick victories against inexperienced competition, but this is not in the long-term interest of the student. As many of the young masters in this book can tell you, it isn't easy to throw away openings that have become useless because opponents don't fall for the tricks. Learning a new set of openings is a lot of work, and a good teacher will build a solid foundation of reliable openings.

A chess coach has a different task. The coach usually works with a student only during a tournament and perhaps for a while before and after the event. There is no time to address many of a player's weaknesses. The coach prepares the student for specific openings and opponents, working within the limitations of the student's ability. The goal is to optimize results in competition, not necessarily to raise the level of the player's game significantly.

A good coach will spend some time working on endgames, because that is the hardest stage of the game to master. The coach will not try to radically change the student's opening repertoire in a short period of time, but will try to patch holes and leaks that could lead to disaster. The coach must also offer psychological support.

Young players often have difficulty rebounding from a bad game and shattered confidence.

Chess training is the most intensive and expensive form of instruction. A trainer provides regular lessons and coaching, and works to eliminate weaknesses and strengthen overall play. Only the most dedicated young players enter chess training programs. Trainers spend a lot of time on subtle positional concepts and endgames. They work to build a complete, solid opening repertoire and sometimes prepare special surprises for specific opponents.

Top trainers rarely impose their own opening strategies on their students. They choose from the entire range of respectable openings, picking some to fit the existing skills of the player, others to bring more experience in areas where improvement is needed. The enormous effort required to train young stars usually results in diminished performances by the trainers, whose rankings can suffer. In any case, the majority of the most successful trainers have been International Masters, not Grandmasters – though some later went on to become Grandmasters. These include Alexander Nikitin (Garry Kasparov), Bob Wade (many English stars), John Watson (Tal Shaked), Igor Zaitsev (Anatoly Karpov).

Some top ranked Grandmasters have become excellent trainers while maintaining their own careers. Josif Dorfman (Etienne Bacrot), Lev Psakhis (Judit Polgar) and Jonathan Speelman (Luke McShane) are good examples. There are even examples of strong players who have almost entirely abandoned competitive play to become full-time trainers, such as Mark Dvoretsky (Artur Jussupow and many others).

Whatever your needs, choosing an appropriate instructor is not an easy task in chess, just as it is hard to select a good music teacher or tennis coach. Still, you can usually find someone in your area who can provide good chess instruction. If you just want to enjoy the game and become a better player, you can play in tournaments and take advantage of some free lessons! Play with opponents who are better than you, and make sure to do a post-mortem (post-game analysis) after every serious game. Of course your "instructors" may not be as qualified as professional trainers, but you are likely to learn some valuable tips. Don't pay too much attention to the opening preferences your opponent might want to foist on you.

Take nothing at face value, but make sure that you understand why your opponent suggests certain moves rather than the ones you played. Perhaps the opponent will be wrong, but there is usually some valuable chess logic to be learned. Naturally, if you get a chance to analyze your game with a strong player, do so! Many scholastic and even open tournaments now offer free analysis of your games by a chess instructor.

When you have played a game and don't understand why you lost, you can also try posting it to the Internet, in the newsgroup rec.games.chess.analysis. Often you'll get several interesting replies, and even Masters answer questions from time to time. Chess lessons are becoming more available on the Internet, too.

RESPONSIBILITIES OF PARENTS, TEACHERS, COACHES AND TRAINERS

Chess players, especially young players, often arrive at a tournament with an entourage, which may include parents, teachers, coaches and trainers. These people can be of great assistance to a player, but must not interfere during a game. The following rules apply strictly in all tournaments:

1. The accompanying persons may not communicate, verbally or otherwise, with the player except in the presence of an arbiter. Any violation of this rule may result in forfeiture of the player.
2. Accompanying persons may not deliver anything to a player during a game. All snacks, medicine or other items must be delivered via an arbiter. Any violation of this rule may result in forfeiture of the player.
3. Accompanying persons are not permitted in the playing area.
4. Accompanying persons may not point out time forfeits or other rule infractions, except by direct communication with the arbiter in a place where the comments cannot be overheard by the players.
5. Accompanying persons may question pairings only until the round has started, and may only discuss pairings with the tournament director or designated assistant. The tournament director is not obliged to offer explanations of pairings.
6. Once the round has started, accompanying persons may not offer advice even if their player has not yet appeared at the board.

7. Photography by accompanying persons is generally restricted to the first five minutes of play, but the tournament director or arbiter may impose other conditions. Accompanying persons do not have the rights of journalists unless their press credentials are accepted by the tournament director in advance of the round.

8. Accompanying persons must remain seated in the designated spectator areas and may not stand in a position which obscures the view of other spectators.

9. Infraction of any of the rules listed above may result in the offender's removal from the playing area. An accompanying person who violates a ban on being present in the playing area may be removed from the tournament venue.

ADDITIONAL RESPONSIBILITIES OF CHESS COACHES

The position of a coach is at times like that of a lawyer, where a member of the bar has overall responsibilities to the legal system. You are there as an advocate for your students, but most importantly, you are there to see that the event is handled with justice.

• Coaches must encourage their players to play fairly.

• Coaches should teach players that it is far better to lose on a touch move call than to be thought a cheater. Even in tender years, a child's reputation is more precious than any game.

• The presence of coaches at an event is primarily to help their players, but a coach may be asked to assist as an arbiter.

• Coaches are forbidden from making a ruling in any game in which one of their players is a participant.

ADDITIONAL RESPONSIBILITIES OF PARENTS AND OTHER SPECTATORS

Rules apply to spectators as well as players. Spectators must remain silent and not interfere with the game. Normally, people watching chess games are reasonably well behaved, though a big electronic 'SILENCE' sign lights frequently during championship competition. When young players compete, it is not the uninvolved spectator that gets in the way, it is usually a parent! Chess parents are a lot like mothers of musical prodigies and young stars in dance and sports.

When they get carried away, they can do some crazy things!

Here are a few examples, with names and details changed to protect the identities of people who, I hope, now realize they should have known better. At one of the World Youth Championships, the weather was unbearably hot and the playing hall was not air conditioned. One of the moms went to the tournament director's office, where the only fan on site was in use. She grabbed it, went into the playing hall, and held the fan so that it cooled her son (and only her son). The tournament officials were not amused.

Parents are usually prohibited from being in the playing area during major competitions (a good thing!), but many will do anything to be able to watch over their children's play. Sometimes they will harangue the operators of the demonstration boards (the oversized chessboards used to display games to the public) and even sometimes force their way in and take over moving the pieces on the demo board, a task for which most parents are horribly ill-suited.

Then there are the parents who are convinced that their children are the next superstars, and they steal the scoresheets, which are the property of the organizers, hoping to auction them off in a few decades for great rewards. Sometimes the theft is not for monetary reasons, but to keep the games from being published, so that future opponents will not be able to prepare effectively.

What happens when a parent and child play in the same tournament? There are many prominent father/son and father/daughter chessplayers (not many mothers in the game, they are too busy!) who travel to tournaments together. Sunil Weeramantry, a FIDE master who is the step-father of young stars Asuka and Hikaru Nakamura, likes to play at a table as far away from his sons as possible, and tries not to be distracted by their games or let them be distracted by his own efforts.

Most organizers would be happier if parents just dropped their kids off at the start of the tournament and picked them up at the end. This used to be normal, but the declining ages of the youngest players and a generally more protective attitude (and even laws!) has made this next to impossible. About the best a young player can do these days is develop a facial expression which lets parents know in no uncertain terms that they should not stay within sight during a game. The distractions have cost far more points than any "help" the parents can provide!

ON KIBITZING

Kibitzing is offering unsolicited advice during a game or post-mortem. During a game it is against the rules. If a player receives advice, the result is likely to be a forfeited game. When someone approaches you during the game and offers a comment on the game, cut them off quickly to avoid getting into trouble.

During a post-mortem, kibitzing may or may not be welcomed by the players. If you saw some important tactic in the game and want to offer advice, it is best to wait until invited to join in. In practice, most people can't resist jumping in, and if you are conducting a post-mortem and don't want kibitzers, do it in private or politely ask on-lookers to leave. The latter rarely happens. A post-mortem is an attempt to find the truth, and sometimes dispassionate onlookers can contribute to the discussion.

When a strong player offers suggestions, you should certainly welcome them. At the Reykjavik international in 1986, Mikhail Tal was in a great mood, and was often helping others with analysis. He even looked at all of my games with me, not just because we were friends (Tal was a friend of almost anyone he ran into frequently), but because the positions were interesting, even if the games were far from perfectly played. Once during the event, American star Yasser Seirawan was conducting a post-mortem with his opponent, also a Grandmaster. When Tal stood by and offered a few comments, Yasser gave up his seat to the former World Champion and remained standing during the analysis!

Although you may think that you and your opponent have worked out all the details, a third party can often spot what you have missed. In one of my games from the Reykjavik tournament, I had a long endgame against a Swedish International Master. During the post-mortem he, and many other strong players, criticized my strategy of playing on opposite wings in an even endgame. By playing with less risk I could have easily drawn the game. True enough, but I have always tried to win against higher rated players. It was one of my best tournaments ever, and I was playing with great confidence. I was sure my strategy was correct. Tal came by and rattled off a fascinating variation, pointing out that I had the right strategy, just not the means to execute it!

Many times outside analysts can shed more light on the game than the players themselves. You don't always appreciate this as you listen in, because the players will often respond to a long tactical variation by implying that they had, of course, considered that plan. Often, this is just a little white lie. No one wants to admit overlooking a tactic!

Take advantage of the opportunities offered by a good public discussion. Put up with a few irrelevant or even stupid comments, because others may be hold great value. Don't hold back too much of your opening analysis. The discussion can find flaws in your logic, and even if a few people know about it, there will be plenty of other opponents to surprise later.

As a kibitzer, try not to annoy the players. Don't point out the obvious, and above all, think before you ask a question or suggest a line! When looking at the opening, it is best to keep quiet. Sometimes you may know of an important recent game in the variation under discussion. Then it is acceptable to mention it. Otherwise, wait until the position has entered the middlegame or endgame. Do not speak to players during the game, and offer no audible comments where you can be heard. Even if the players seem to be just playing blitz for fun, there may be stakes involved and kibitzing during blitz games is never welcome.

XI. THE TOURNAMENT DIRECTOR

The tournament director is responsible for all aspects of the tournament except enforcement of the rules, which is the duty of the Arbiter. In the United States Chess Federation, no distinction is made between arbiters and tournament directors, but in most of the world, the duties are strictly separate. One way to understand the respective duties is to consider everything that goes on inside the tournament hall (playing area) belongs to the arbiter, and everything outside to the tournament director.

The tournament director is often the organizer of the event, or may be an individual who works for the organizer. Among the most important tasks of the tournament director are:
- Keeping track of all of the tournament entries.
- Making all arrangements with the venue and tournament hotel.
- Preparing and distributing schedules.
- Preparing the pairings for each round.
- Arranging facilities for the press.
- Dealing with all complaints from players, coaches, trainers etc.

RESOLVING DISPUTES

Each tournament should have an appeal committee, designated by the tournament director before the start of the event. In the event of a dispute, a player may make an appeal to the committee. The appeal must be made in writing prior to the scheduled start of the following round, or, in the case of the last round of a tournament, within 2 hours after the conclusion of play. The tournament may require a cash deposit, which will be returned if the appeal is granted but forfeited if the claim is denied. This deposit should be proportional to the prize fund of the event, perhaps one or two percent of the first prize.

PAIRING PROBLEMS

Computer-generated pairings are thoroughly objective but can sometimes produce pairings which may be undesirable, for example pairing family members against each other, or matching students against their trainers. The tournament director has the right to override the computer when a pairing creates an undesirable situation, but the director must have guidelines in place so that such changes do not seem arbitrary. In professional competition, changes to computer pairings are only justified when the pairing is incorrect, but for amateur and scholastic events, more flexibility can be applied.

When making manual pairings, the tournament director has more discretion, and should strive for fairness above all else. Standard pairing rules should be followed whenever possible.

Once the pairings are posted, changes should be made only:

1. When the pairings are incorrect because a result in the previous round was incorrectly reported (all events)
2. If it is discovered that two family members have been paired against each other (amateur and scholastic only)
3. If it is discovered that a player has been paired against their teacher or trainer (amateur and scholastic only)

In the case changes are needed, they should be made before the round begins. The preferred change is to switch the opponent to that of the nearest board where the higher rated player is due for the same color.

In other words, assume that player A, rated 1800, is paired against player B, rated 1500. Before the round begins, it is discovered that this pairing is incorrect (for example, perhaps the players have already faced each other)

Player	Rating
A	1800
B	1500
C	1700
D	1400
E	1300
F	1600

The quickest change is to switch player B with Player D, who is scheduled to play Black. It would not be correct to switch B with F, because player F is the higher rated player in that game. It would not be correct to switch B with E because that would affect the colors.

This is illustrated here.

Board	White	Black
1	A	B
2	E	F
3	C	D

changes to

Board	White	Black
1	A	D
2	E	F
3	C	B

When the pairing is incorrect because a wrong score was entered in the computer, whether the error was made by a player or a staff member, pairings should be redone if sufficient time permits. When computers are used, this can be done so quickly that even if the round is about to begin, the pairings can be changed. If, however, the error is noticed so late that changes are not possible without significantly delaying the round, or if manual pairings are used, then pairing should not be done. Instead, the tournament director should make the minimal change necessary so that each player plays within the proper score group.

XII. RESPONSIBILITIES OF THE PLAYERS

Players are required to:

1. Obey the Rules of Chess at all times.
2. Treat the Arbiter, Tournament Director, and all event staff with courtesy and respect.
3. Behave properly toward all other competitors.
4. To properly record the result of each game on the pairing sheet or result slip.
5. To dress appropriately for the competition.

XIII. THE CHESS EDUCATION ASSOCIATION

The Chess Education Association is a non-profit corporation overseeing scholastic chess activities. It is dedicated to providing scholastic chess to the widest possible number of students and providing competitive and educational activities for its players.

Early in 1999, several well-known coaches met to address the needs of the scholastic chess community so that the chessplayers of the 21st century would be able to receive assistance without the onerous burden of a dues structure, which had kept many needy children from participating in organized chess. Sunil Weeramantry, Dewain Barber, Al Woolum, John Surlow, David Lither, and Richard Peterson joined forces to produce a free online scholastic chess website. The result was the introduction of ChessLogic.com in November of 1999.

This website provides resources for young chess players, their parents and coaches, and a coordinated rating system which allows young players to measure their progress. It also provides a forum for kids to share their experiences with their peers.

The goal of the CEA is to encourage more chess in our schools, and to teach children positive life values through the chess experience. There is no charge for membership in the CEA.

QUESTIONS AND ANSWERS ABOUT SCHOLASTIC CHESS

Why does scholastic chess need it's own set of rules?

Because of the concentration on scholastic chess, since many of the players are new to the game, our coaches felt it was necessary to have a set of rules designed only for young and predominately new players.

Is it true that the Arbiter may intercede in a CEA game?

Yes, he can. This is one of the big differences between the adult chess rules and the scholastic rules. Under the adult rules, a young player had to know all of the myriad rules himself. Further, you had to know how to apply the rules. We felt that was too much to ask of a young player. In the scholastic system, the arbiter can step in to help.

Can the Arbiter declare a game won by a player when the opponent exceeds the time limit?

Yes, it is a subtle distinction, but under CEA rules the arbiter is a part of the game. Except for the USCF tournaments, this is the rule in the rest of the world.

May a parent announce a time forfeit?

Absolutely not. Parents are not a part of the game and should remain silent during the competition. Further, they should stand behind their players and avoid eye contact.

What happens if I see an illegal move?

Absolutely nothing. You are an observer of the game, not a participant.

SCHOLASTIC CHESS TOURNAMENTS
Registration

It is best to pre-register for chess tournaments and to provide the proper ID. That way, a tournament director can get the player correctly listed in his database of players for that event and post an alphabetical listing of all players in the relevant sections.

It is important for players to know the time control of their tournament so that their clock is properly set and to listen carefully to announcements for any relevant information including rules variations. For instance, if a player does not know how to report results, that player might not be paired for the next game.

Pairings

Pairings should be posted in a spacious area where there is no crowding. Considering the number of players, multiple postings of the pairings should be considered. The pairings are generally posted two different ways. Alphabetical listings which will show opponent, board number, and color and board order lists starting with Board 1. These often are used for result sheets as well.

Results are normally recorded by the tournament director after collecting the signed scoresheets, but in some events, particularly in USCF events, players are responsible for marking the results on the pairing charts. Failure to record the results properly can result in a double forfeit, where both players lose the game. An incorrectly reported result can drastically affect future pairings and is a common problem at large amateur events where players are responsible for reporting results.

Alphabetical Pairing Chart

Name	Color	Opponent	Board
Harutyun Akopyan	White	David Petty	2
Manuel Alfaro	Black	Aaron Schacht	21
Vinay Bhat	Black	David Karapetian	1
Benli Cai	Black	Antonio Sanchez	14
William Chang		Unpaired	
Gabriele Cook		Full Point Bye	
Jack Curry	White	Garrett Wittwer	22
Scott Donato	White	Dustin Kerksieck	18
Eric England	Black	Kevin Simler	11
Andrew Fan	White	Ernest Huang	8
Micah Fisher-Kirschner	Black	Simion Kreimer	3
Jeremy Fremlin	Black	Edvoud Guevorkia	13
Sergey Frenklakh	White	Jayodita Songhri	12

Pairing Chart in Board Order

			Name			Opponent
1	24	___	Jeremy Fremlin	1	___	Vinay Bhat
2	2	___	Harutyun Akopyan	25	___	Garrett Wittwer
3	26	___	Ruben Salazar	3	___	M.Fisher-Kirschner
4	4	___	David Karapetian	27	___	P. Perepelitsky
5	28	___	Manuel Alfaro	5	___	Andrew Fan
6	6	___	Kris Maclennan	29	___	Jack Curry
7	30	___	Oliver Kong	7	___	A. Varuzhanyan
8	8	___	Simion Kreimer	31	___	Jayodita Songhri
9	32	___	Jason Mar	9	___	David Petty
10	10	___	Joseph Lonsdale	33	___	Eric England
11	34	___	Daniel Scherbakovs	11	___	Prashant Periwal
12	12	___	Kevin Simler	35	___	Aaron Blavin
13	36	___	Edvoud Guevorkian	13	___	Sergey Frenklakh
14	14	___	Jeff Kottcamp	37	___	Hai Nguyen
15	38	___	Marcus Yip	15	___	Nicholas Gilbert
16	16	___	Jocelyn Lee	39	___	William Chang

Here is how pairings work, as used in CEA events. Suppose that we have 12 players register for a tournament. The 12 players are rated in order from the highest rated down to the lowest rated. If an event is based on a rating system where unrated players are present, the unrated players are placed at the bottom, in alphabetical order. The CEA does not have unrated players but instead assigns a rating based on age as described earlier.

The players are divided into two groups with the six highest (top half) playing the six lowest (bottom half). Player #1 will play player #7, player #2 will play player #8, and so on down to player # 6 playing player #12.

After the first game, scores are recorded for each player. Let us assume that players ranked #1 through #6 all won their games. In the 1-0 group, the second round pairings are: player #1 will play player #4, player #2 will play player number 5, etc. In the 0-1 group, player #7 will play player #10. Player #8 will play player #11.

If there are an even number of players, then everyone will play. No one is eliminated from the competition because of losses. If there are an odd number of players, the lowest rated player in the lowest score group will be awarded a full point bye.

Colors

In a perfect world, players would alternate colors every other game. Unfortunately, it is not a perfect world. Suppose in our example above that all of the players with the White pieces won their first round games. The tournament director is then faced with the problem of pairing six players who are all due Black. The three highest rated players who are due Black will be given Black while the other three players will play Black in the next game. A player will never play the same color in three successive rounds.

Rounds

Round times should be posted in the same area as the postings and should be adhered to as closely as possible by the tournament staff and players.

Reporting Results

Players will be advised how to report game results. All players are responsible for reporting results, regardless of the outcome of the game.

If for some reason your opponent did not appear and you have earned a forfeit win, please make sure the scorers understand that your win was by forfeit. The only thing worse than sitting and waiting for someone who is not coming is for that person to have forfeited the prior round with the tournament directors not knowing to delete him or her from the database.

SCHOOL TEAMS AND CLUB TEAMS

School Teams

A *school* is defined as one campus with one principal or equivalent. For instance, Desert Shadows Elementary may be immediately adjacent to Desert Shadows Middle School, but if they each have their own principal, then they are not one school and players from the Desert Shadows Elementary may not play on the Desert Shadows Middle School team.

A school is further defined by its highest grade. For instance, Desert Shadows Elementary is a K-6 school. It may not ever compete as a K-5 school. Another example; Desert Shadows Elementary is a K-5 school. Desert Shadows Middle School is 6-8.

Desert Shadows Elementary is only eligible to compete as a K-5 school. If 6th graders from Desert Shadows Middle School wish to compete in the elementary section, they must compete on their own middle school team or as members of a club team. They may not compete for Desert Shadows Elementary School.

A *school team* is defined by three or more players from the same school competing in the same section of a tournament. For instance, if three players from Desert Shadows Elementary are playing in the elementary section of the state championship, then Desert Shadows has a school team.

If two players from Desert Shadows were playing, then they would not be a school team and would then be eligible to compete on a club team.

Club Teams

A club team is a group of players from different schools with no more than two players from any one school, who have registered as a club prior to the start of the first round. Players may not change their club registration status after the start of the first round. It is up to the club members or their coach to make sure they are properly registered.

Elective Divisions

CEA rules have a clear prejudice against schools with large numbers of grades to exploit, so for instance, a young star could play on the high school team for 10 years if he had the talent. To remedy this situation, the CEA developed the "elective division."

Some small schools (usually K-8 or K-12) otherwise stuck with odd grade levels may choose to do an elective division. Once chosen, however, this division will be considered permanent. For instance, a school that is split K-4, 5-8, and 9-12 may chose to be split K-3, 4-6, 7-8, 9-12. The redivision of the school must contain one more divide than the original school configuration. This is completely elective and must be accompanied by a letter from the chief administrative officer of the school stating that this election is voluntary and permanent. Otherwise, the standard rules apply. In the example given, after the elective division a fourth grader could only play on the 4-6 team and a seventh grader could only play on the 7-8 team.

General Rules for Teams

Neither schools nor clubs are limited as to the number of players who participate, however in national competitions where there are multiple grade championships (such as the CEA National Elementary, or CEA National High School) the top four scores from each team shall represent the team score. In national competitions where each grade is competing only against itself, then teams shall consist of the top three scorers from each team.

Generally, teammates do not play each other. However, there are exceptions.

1. First, if the players in the top score group are all from the same school, then pairing them is inevitable and will be done.

2. Second, if one school has a large percentage of the total number of players in a section, then that school's players will be required to play each other in the lower half of the score groups.

3. Third, if in the sole determination of the chief tournament director, the apparent strength of the players on a club team may negatively effect the competitive balance of the tournament as a whole, then the tournament director may choose to alter the pairings.

In this manner, club players may be forced to play each other while still representing their clubs for the final team standings.

Occasionally, an error is made in scoring a round and two opposing players are given the wrong scores. The result of this error is that one player plays up in a higher score group when he or she should be playing in a lower score group. The reverse is true of the other player who should be playing in the higher score group, but receives the benefit of playing in a lower score group.

This causes severe problems, especially when claims for reversal of the error are made in later rounds or worse, when the tournament is over. For instance, a player could have had a scoring error in round 2, but then had the benefit of the lower pairings for every succeeding round. These errors are called "pocket points."

CEA rules make these errors the responsibility of the coaches and the players. No scoring errors will be changed later than two rounds after the error occurred if the error happened on the same calendar day. If the error occurred during the last round played on a calendar day, then the error must be corrected before the start of the second round on the following calendar day. Here are two examples. Player A defeats Player B in the first round, but it is accidentally scored as a win for Player B. The error must be reported prior to the end of round 3 in order for the score to be changed. On the same calendar day, you have two rounds to correct the error.

Player A defeats Player B in the last round on Saturday, but it is accidentally scored as a win for Player B. The error must be reported prior to the start of the second round on Sunday for the scoring error to be corrected. When the error occurs on one calendar day and the next game is on the next calendar day, then you must report the error prior to the start of the second round.

The following is the rationale. Over a large number of rounds in a swiss tournament, players will come close to their own true score, even if a scoring error has been made in a prior round. For instance, if a player in round three is scored as a loss when he has really won, then he will receive lower pairings (an easier opponent) for his next round. If he had been paired properly, he would have played a player with a higher score (a tougher opponent). In spite of this, over the course of a tournament he will return to his true pairing group and his final score will nearly (not perfectly) reflect his performance.

This is certainly a fairer result than giving a full point in a later round or worse, when the tournament is over. For instance, if a player scored six points, but only five points were scored on the wall chart, that player scored those six points against weaker opponents than other players in the six point group.

RESPONSIBILITIES OF CHESS PARENTS AT SCHOLASTIC TOURNAMENTS

- Encourage your players to play fairly.
- Every game of chess is an ethics lesson.
- Do not interfere in your children's games. If you do, then your child could lose because of your action. The games are between the kids. Only the arbiter may intervene.
- The greatest learning experience for our players takes place over the chessboard at the peer level without parental involvement.
- Be sure your kids have something to eat and drink during the tournament.
- Bring a book or something to occupy your time.
- Don't mention another appointment or put your kids in time pressure away from the board. It is better to request a bye than have a child play at a mental disadvantage.
- Let the tournament organizer know as early as possible if your child cannot participate in a scheduled game.

NO VIOLENCE POLICY

The Chess Education Association has a no violence policy. This extends beyond the children to the parents and coaches as well. Violence (this includes spanking) is not allowed at any CEA event under any circumstances and will result in the immediate expulsion of the player and/or parent or coach from that event. It is unfortunate that a rule like this is necessary, but the CEA is working very hard for the welfare of children.

Event expulsion is not meant to be punitive. It is meant to be protective. It is hoped that expulsion from the event may allow the parties involved to think better of their public actions and provide a cooling off period. Repeated violations will result in expulsion from all CEA events.

IV. SELECTED RESOURCES

WEBSITES

The Internet is constantly changing and websites come and go. We cannot guarantee that the following web sites will still be there when you go to take a look, but here are some of the most useful sites. There are thousands of chess websites, and the ones listed are simply those which are most relevant to the topics discussed in this book. Updated links are available at Chess City, www.chesscity.com.

Chess City Magazine

Chess City Magazine, www.chesscity.com, is owned and operated by Cardoza Publishing, part of the Cardoza family which includes the publisher of this book. Eric Schiller is the editor. This is an all-purpose chess site which is geared primarily toward amateur players. You can find chess instruction and analysis, book and software information, photos, trivia, stories, and all sorts of goodies there.

ChessLogic

This is the home of the Chess Education Association. www.chesslogic.com is a free website that ties all the CEA events around the country together. ChessLogic combines the functions of the CEA online magazine, the free Scholastic Chess Webzine including chess archives, a free rating service which shows the top 100 lists for every grade and every age in every state as well as nationally, and free tournament announcements with state and national listings. It is also the initial registration point for players, coaches, and interested parents. A tournament director using Swiss Sys pairing software can instantly upload the results and the players can see their rating changes reflected on the updated Top 100 lists.

Braingames Network

The Braingames Network is a new organization that was put together to run World Championship and other competitions in a variety of mind sports. Their website is www.braingames.net, where you can find information about ongoing and future events. Braingames sponsored the 2000 World Championship match between Garry Kasparov and Vladimir Kramnik, which resulted in Kramnik's becoming the 14th World Chess Champion.

The Week in Chess

Mark Crowther edits the essential weekly web publication *The Week in Chess*, located at www.chesscenter.com/twic/twic.html. TWIC covers all major events in the world of chess and acts as a repository for chess news and a selection of the most important chess games played each week.

F.I.D.E.

The *Federation Internationale des Echecs* is a worldwide organization with over 150 national chess federations affiliated. It organizes the Chess Olympiads, World Youth Championships and many other international events. The website www.fide.com has a great deal of information about International Chess. From 1948 to 1990, FIDE organized the official World Chess Championship. Since 1993, when World Champion Kasparov broke with the group, FIDE has organized its own world championships, though these are not generally recognized by the media or chess playing public. Nevertheless, FIDE is recognized by the International Olympic Committee as the international governing body for chess.

World Blitz Chess Association

American Grandmaster Walter Browne founded and still runs the WBCA, which is dedicated to chess played at a rate of 5 minutes per player per game. The WBCA maintains a website at members.aol.com/wbcablitz.

Australian Chess Federation

www.somerset.qld.edu.au/chess/

British Chess Federation

www.bcf.ndirect.co.uk/

Canadian Chess Federation
www.chess.ca/chess.html

United States Chess Federation
The United States Chess Federation maintains an extensive website at www.uschess.com. Although the authors have a rather low opinion of their specific rules, this organization can provide invaluable information on tournament chess in the United States and is well worth visiting. If you plan to play tournament chess in the U.S., or compete in international competition as an American, membership, currently at $40 per year, is mandatory.

Other Resources
www.swissperfect.com(home of Swiss Perfect pairing software)
www.chessclub.com(Internet Chess Club)
www.swisssys.com(SwissSys)

APPENDIX A: PAIRING SYSTEMS

ROUND ROBIN PAIRINGS

Round Robin pairings are the easiest to do by hand. Just assign each player a number (usually by random drawing) and then use the pairing tables. Pairing numbers are usually assigned by lottery. The tables below show the pairings for round robin events.

If there is an odd number of players, then the highest number (e.g., 4, in a quadrangular) is replaced by a "Bye." In all tables, the player of the White side is listed first.

If the event is a double round-robin, the second set of games is played with the opposite color assignments. The games may then be played as two cycles, or as mini-matches, where the players have a rematch with opposite colors after the first game is complete. The latter is the preferred format, since it is more efficient in terms of scheduling, especially in rapid chess events.

3-4 Players "Quad"

Round	Board 1	Board 2
1	1:4	2:3
2	4:3	2:1
3	2:4	3:1

5-6 Players "Hexagon"

Round	Board 1	Board 2	Board 3
1	1:6	2:5	3:4
2	6:4	5:3	1:2
3	2:6	3:1	4:5
4	6:5	1:4	2:3
5	3:6	4:2	5:1

7-8 Players "Octagon"

Round	Board 1	Board 21	Board 3	Board 4
1	1:8	2:7	3:6	4:5
2	8:5	6:4	7:3	1:2
3	2:8	3:1	4:7	5:6
4	8:6	7:5	1:4	2:3
5	3:8	4:2	5:1	6:7
6	8:7	1:6	2:5	3:4
7	4:8	5:3	6:2	7:1

9-10 Players "Decagon"

Round	Board 1	Board 2	Board 3	Board 4	Board 5
1	1:10	2:9	3:8	4:7	5:6
2	10:6	7:5	8:4	9:3	1:2
3	2:10	3:1	4:9	5:8	6:7
4	10:7	8:6	9:5	1:4	2:3
5	3:10	4:2	5:1	6:9	7:8
6	10:8	9:7	1:6	2:5	3:4
7	4:10	5:3	6:2	7:1	8:9
8	10:9	1:8	2:7	3:6	4:5
9	5:10	6:4	7:3	8:2	9:1

Additional charts for larger tournaments can be found at our website, www.chesscity.com.

Note that if the tournament is a double-round robin, the order of the final two rounds is reversed in order to avoid any player having to play as Black three times in a row.

SCHEVENINGEN PAIRINGS

Scheveningen pairings are used in matches between two teams. To calculate the pairings for a Schevingen system, start by deciding which of the two teams have White. This is usually done by a lottery, such as a coin toss. In the first round, the players on each team play against the player on the opposite team who is on the same rank within the team. The top ranked player of team A plays against the top ranked player of team B and the second ranked player of team A plays against the second ranked player of team B, and so on. The top rated player on each team is assigned number 1 with the others following in rating order.

In each subsequent round, the player of team A faces the player on team B ranked one level lower. So in round 2, team A's top player faces the second-ranked player on team B. The players alternate colors, so if the team A player has White in the first round, that player will have Black in the next round. After playing the lowest ranked player on an opposing team, the player shifts to the top player and works downward. The chart below shows these pairings.

Scheveningen Pairings

Team A Player	Has Color	in Round	vs.	Team B Player
1,3,5,7...	White	1		1,3,5,7...
2,4,6,8....	Black	1		2,4,6,8...
1,3,5,7...	Black	2		2,4,6,8...
2,4,6,8....	White	2		3,5,7,1...
1,3,5,7...	White	3		3,5,7,1...
2,4,6,8....	Black	3		4,6,8,2...
1,3,5,7...	Black	4		4,6,8,2...
2,4,6,8....	White	4		5,7,1,3...
1,3,5,7...	White	5		5,7,1,3...
2,4,6,8....	Black	5		6,8,2,4...
1,3,5,7...	Black	6		6,8,2,4...
2,4,6,8...	White	6		7,1,3,5...
1,3,5,7...	White	7		7,1,3,5
2,4,6,8....	Black	7		8,2,4,6
1,3,5,7...	Black	8		8,2,4,6
2,4,6,8...	White	8		1,3,5,7

SWISS SYSTEM

In modern times, the Swiss System is almost always implemented by computer programs. We recommend two such programs. To be more precise, Eric Schiller endorses the Swiss Perfect program (www.swissperfect.com) for use in professional and amateur events, and the Chess Education Association endorses the Swiss Sys program (www.swisssys.com) for use in scholastic events. Information about these two programs can be found at their respective websites. There are other pairing programs, and most of them will do the job adequately. The differences relate primarily to fine points of adjusting for colors and equalizing score groups, as well as other minor algorithmic matters. For online play, the Internet Chess Club uses special software, known as Tomato, for administering Swiss system tournaments including all pairings.

APPENDIX B: BRAINGAMES.NET WORLD CHESS CHAMPIONSHIP REGULATIONS

The World Chess Championship has been held under the auspices of many different individuals and organizations. The history of the event is a complicated affair, but it is generally accepted that the title was established in the 1886 match between Steinitz and Zukertort, held in various cities in the United States.

The title passed from champion to champion in match competition until 1948 when, after the death of titleholder Alexander Alekhine, it was administered by FIDE, the World Chess Federation, until 1993. In that year, World Champion Garry Kasparov, unhappy with the conditions imposed by the multinational organization, transferred the title to the short-lived Professional Chess Association.

After the demise of that organization, the Braingames Network stepped in with a two million dollar prize for the 2000 match against the undisputed number one contender Vladimir Kramnik, held in London. Below is an edited version of those regulations.

1. STRUCTURE OF THE MATCH
1. The match shall consist of 16 games, with players alternating colors each round.
2. The winner of the match is the player who scores 8.5 or more points.
3. In the event of a tie, the title is retained by the Champion, and the prize fund is divided equally.

2. PRIZES
1. The prize fund for the match is two million US Dollars, with 2/3 going to the winner and 1/3 to the loser.

3. SCHEDULE

Games will be played at 3:00 PM at the Riverside Television Studios, Hammersmith, London, on Sundays, Tuesdays, Thursdays and Saturdays from October 8, 2000 through November 4, 2000.

4. TOURNAMENT DIRECTOR

The tournament director for the match is Raymond Keene. The responsibility of the tournament director covers all aspects of the match not specifically delegated to the players, arbiters or match committee.

5. MATCH COMMITTEE

1.   The match committee is responsible for ruling on appeals from delegations concerning the decisions of the arbiter or organizers.
2.   If a player wishes to appeal a decision, or make some other official complaint, the player or his official representative must submit a written appeal specifying the issue under dispute, the official ruling, and any comments or criticisms of that ruling, together with a requested specific remedy. A deposit of $500, which shall be refunded unless the match committee rules that the appeal is utterly without merit.
3.   The appeal should be filed as quickly as possible, but in any case not later than two hours following the conclusion of the game in which the incident occurred. If the incident occurred outside of a match game, the appeal must be filed not more than six hours before the scheduled start of the game, unless circumstances make that impossible.
4.   A quorum of three members is required for any action to be voted upon, including at least one of the two Grandmasters.

The match committee consists of :
Chairman: Tony Buzan (England)
Deputy Chairman: Lord Hardinge (Scotland)
Grandmaster Lothar Schmid (Germany)
Grandmaster Fridrik Olafsson (Iceland)
His Excellency Yousuf Shirawi (Bahrain)

Henry Mutkin (England), non-voting Secretary

6. ARBITERS
The arbiters for the match are
  Yuri Averbakh (Russia)
  Andrzej Filipowicz (Poland)
  Eric Schiller (USA)
Two of these three will be on duty at all times while a game is in progress. Mr. Filipowicz will act as Chief Arbiter.
The duties of the arbiter include:
1. Securing and checking the playing equipment and playing site
2. Setting and verifying the proper functioning of the chess clock
3. Check that the demonstration boards are properly set up and functioning
4. Check each of the player's private on-stage rooms and the toilets.
5. At least one arbiter shall be present at the playing venue 30 minutes prior to the scheduled start of the game, to deal with any issues that may arise.
6. During the game, insure that all of the rules and regulations of the match are enforced
7. At least two arbiters shall be on duty at any time when a game in progress.
8. At least one arbiter shall be present on stage at all times during the game.
9. At least one arbiter shall remain in the venue for 15 minutes after the conclusion of play, to deal with any issues that may arise.
10. Arbiters will dress properly, i.e. in jackets and ties and suitable other garments, at all times when they are on duty.
11. Arbiters shall take no action to influence the result of any game, nor will they do anything to distract the players save when required to act by the rules and regulations.
12. Arbiters shall take action as required to reduce or eliminate noise in the playing hall.
13. Arbiters shall cooperate with security personnel to identify spectators who have violated rules.

7. TIME CONTROL

The time control of the Braingames.Net World Chess Championship is 40 moves in 120 minutes, followed by 20 moves in 60 minutes, followed by all moves in 30 minutes plus ten seconds per move, non-accumulating, added prior to the move.

For the purposes of enforcing rules which apply when a player in is time pressure:

1. If only one player has less than 5 minutes remaining, that player is in a state of time pressure.
2. If both player have less than 5 minutes remaining, the players are in a state of mutual time pressure.
3. If either player has less than one minute remaining, the game is in a state of extreme time pressure.

8. SPECIFIC PENALTIES

For the following specific rule violations, the offending party shall be notified in the instance of the first transgression of a rule. A second transgression of the same rule shall result in the offending party receiving an official warning. A third transgression results in the loss of the game.

1. A player who has more than 5 minutes time remaining fails to record his opponent's previous move on the scoresheet prior to completing his current move, when the opponent has less than 5 minutes time remaining.
2. A player who has more than 5 minutes time remaining causes his opponent to be distracted when the opponent has less than 5 minutes time remaining.
3. . A player who has more than 5 minutes time remaining causes his opponent to be distracted when the opponent has more than 5 minutes time remaining.}

All circumstances not addressed here remain within the scope of the arbiter's discretion.

9. EQUIPMENT

1. The DGT digital clock will be used in the World Championship match.
2. The player of the White pieces will be on the stage right/left side of the table, so that the clock faces toward/away from the audience.

10. PLAYING CONDITIONS

1. The chairs, chessboard, scoresheets, pieces, tables and clocks shall be approved by each delegation.
2. The arrangement of the abovementioned items and the toilet and refreshment facilities shall be approved by each delegation.
3. Lighting shall be approved by each delegation
4. The players will review the arrangements listed in points 1-3 on Friday, October 5, at a time to be determined.
5. Spectators shall be located as indicated in the approved floor plan.
6. Spectators who interfere with play in any way will be removed from the playing hall as quickly as possible.
7. Only the players and arbiters can be on the stage during play.
8. Metal detectors will be used in the venue for spectators and players.
9. Mobile phones will be banned from the playing hall completely. An announcement will be made before each game that mobile phones, pagers and beepers shall be switched off.
10. High level of security backstage.
11. Players agree to undergo a personal search prior to the start of each game.
12. Player's delegations and guests will be seated in reserved seats where eye contact with their player will not be possible.

11. TOILET AND REFRESHMENT FACILITIES

1. Toilet facilities shall be approved by the players prior to the start of the match.
2. Player's side rooms will be provided with chair, monitor showing current position of the game and refreshments. For each game, the player of the White pieces will use the room located off-stage on the side closest to the player, and the player of the Black pieces will use the room located off-stage on the side closes to him.
3. The arbiter may enter the private areas.

THE OFFICIAL RULES OF CHESS • CARDOZA PUBLISHING

4. The organizers will place security cameras in the private rooms, but not in the toilet facilities.
5. Players will each have a dressing room. This room will be locked during play. Before and after each game players and delegations may have access.

12. PLAYER RESPONSIBILITIES

1. Players will wear appropriate attire during all games, ceremonies and press functions, including jackets and ties. Players may remove jackets and ties during play, but may not remove other items of clothing.
2. Players shall make every effort to arrive punctually for all games and official events.

13. DRAWING OF LOTS

First, the Champion shall choose one of two identical objects. One of the two objects will confer the right to choose the next lot.

Second, the winner of the first lot will choose one of two identical objects from the Staunton Cup. One will indicate that the holder will play the White side in the first game, and the other will indicate that the holder will play the Black side in the first game

14. OPENING AND CLOSING CEREMONIES

The players are obliged to be at both events, which will be scheduled in the evening. The opening ceremony will not take place the evening before the first round unless absolutely necessary.

1. Opening ceremony will take place October 5 at 6:30 PM in the Home House, 20 Portman Square, London W1H.
2. Closing ceremony will take place November 5 at a time and place to be determined by the organizers.

15. PRESS CONFERENCES

1. The opening press conference will be on the morning of the opening ceremony.
2. There will be a press photo opportunity at 3:00 PM at the playing venue.
3. Post game conferences will be attended by both players however either player shall have the right to give a separate conference.

4. Post-game press conferences will be limited to ten minutes, as a goal, with an absolute maximum of 15 minutes unless one or both players agree to extend it for a few additional minutes.

16. PHOTOGRAPHY

1. Photographs and other video recording will be permitted during the first 5 minutes of the first game
2. In all subsequent games for 3 minutes after both players have arrived at the table.
3. Web cams providing authorized transmissions may be active at all times.

17. ILLNESS AND CIRCUMSTANCES BEYOND THE CONTROL OF THE ORGANIZERS

1. If a player is unable to complete or play a game due to illness, the player shall forfeit the game.
2. In the event a game is canceled due to reasons beyond the control of the organizers, it shall be rescheduled for two days after the final scheduled game of the match.
3. In the event a game in progress must be interrupted for reasons of health, security or in the event of power failure, the arbiters shall determine the appropriate action depending on the circumstances. The players may appeal this decision at any time prior to the resumption of play, or within four hours should the arbiters decide to annul the game.

18. OFFICIAL LANGUAGE

The official language for all rules, regulations and agreements is English. The Arbiters can also communicate with the players in Russian, should that be necessary.

APPENDIX C: A FEW WORDS ON USCF RULES

American players who have appeared in a tournament organized by the United States Chess Federation will no doubt have noticed that there are some significant differences between the rules presented here and those they have encountered in those tournaments. Those interested in the particular rules used by the United States Chess Federation should consult the U.S.C.F. rulebook.

The problem with the USCF rules is that they are designed primarily for the benefit of organizers, not players. Those rules require the players to act as their own referees in many cases. For example, you cannot claim a win by time forfeit unless you have a complete and legible scoresheet (and there is little agreement on exactly what that is). In general, the idea is to minimize the need for arbiters and thus maximize revenues for event organizers. These provincial rules are not in force anywhere else in the known universe, and players who grow up using them often encounter difficulties when playing abroad.

To give the reader an idea of the absurdity of some of these rules, let us provide a simple example. In a USCF tournament a player can actually chose the time control of the game! In order to maximize profits, most USCF tournament provide no playing equipment (sets, boards or clocks). Their rule is that the player of the Black pieces has choice over the equipment. If a digital clock is used, then the time control must involve an increment, so that instead of one hour the player has, say, 50 minutes plus five seconds per move. But if a traditional analog clock is used, the time control is one hour with no increment. A player who owns both clocks can actually choose the control by bringing only the desired clock to the game.

The USCF excuses these strange rules by stating that in large tournaments it is impossible (read: too expensive) to supply a sufficient number of arbiters. However, as the rest of the world knows, in most cases the arbiter is only needed in case of time pressure, and in this case it is easy enough to find volunteers to act as witnesses and report the facts of any dispute to an arbiter.

Since only a small percentage of American chessplayers actually play in USCF events, the authors find no need to discuss these rules in detail. In any case, the USCF rules are constantly undergoing revision, and should you find yourself playing in such an event you should ask the tournament director to explain the differences between the USCF rules and the standard (international) rules.

LAST WORDS

We hope that this book holds all the answers to your questions about the rules of chess, whether played casually or in competition for a championship title. As in most sports, the rules and regulations change, so it is important to keep up-to-date. You can visit Chess City Magazine, our website, to see changes as they are introduced.

Just as this book was going to press, FIDE announced a radical proposal to change the time control so that games will end in less than four hours. Although FIDE seems determined to increase the pace of play, strenuous objections were raised by both players and national chess organizations, and it is too soon to tell whether the change will actually be implemented.

Most major chess organizations have standing committees to evaluate and refine the rules. Most rule changes are minor, however. If you understand the rules as presented in this book you can feel confident that you can play chess in almost any tournament without having to make adjustments. Remember to ask about any deviations from the standard rules, because in the vast majority of tournaments, very little effort is made to explain them.

Good luck, and enjoy your chess, whether it is played on the World Championship stage, in a park, or in cyberspace!